THE BUILDING OF THE KOSMOS

THE BUILDING OF THE KOSMOS

And Other Lectures Delivered at the Eighteenth Annual Convention of the Theosophical Society at Adyar, Madras, December 27th, 28th, 29th, 30th, 1893

BY

ANNIE BESANT

GYAN

ISBN: 978-81-212-1922-8 (HB)
First Published, 1894
Published, 2018
Published by

Gyan Publishing House
5, Ansari Road
Daryaganj, New Delhi-110002
Phone: 011-47034999, 9811692060
www.gyanbooks.com
E-mail: books@gyanbooks.com

Printed at: G. Print Process, Delhi.

CONTENTS.

PREFACE.

THE four lectures printed in this volume were delivered to the delegates and members of the Theosophical Society, assembled for the Annual Convention at Adyar, Madras, on December 27th, 28th, 29th, 30th, 1893. They were intended to show the value of the teachings of H. P. Blavatsky as a guide to the obscurer meanings of the Hindû Sacred books, and so to vindicate at once the usefulness of the Theosophical and the Hindû doctrines. They were intended also to show the identity of these doctrines, and to prove that any one who believes the Theosophical teachings must accept those of the *Vedas* and the *Purânas* on fundamental matters. That Theosophy is a fragment of the Brahma Vidyâ of pre-Vaidic days, that the Shruti are the best exoteric presentment of Brahma Vidyâ, that the *Purânas* were intended to give to the class excluded from the study of the *Vedas* the spiritual truths contained in the latter in a concrete form easy of assimilation—such were the ideas which sought expression in these lectures.

My acceptance of Theosophical teachings has to me, from the beginning, implied the acceptance of the Hindû Scriptures as the mine out of which the gold of Spiritual Knowledge was to be dug. As a Philosophy, Theosophy may be held intellectually apart from Hindûism as from all Religions, though reproducing on many points the Advaita Vedânta; but if any attempt be made to draw from it spiritual sustenance, if it be taught as Religion as well as Philosophy, then in the Hindûism which is its earliest and fullest exoteric presentment will the need for worship find its completest satisfaction. I do not mean that devotion may not clothe itself in various religious garbs; and that if a man have a Religion when he becomes a Theosophist, he will not naturally seek in that Religion the spiritual food he requires and will not therein find it. But if he comes into Theosophy, as I did, from Materialism, then he will most probably in his devotion adopt the ancient Sanskrit forms preserved in Hindûism, with which he has become intellectually familiar in his philosophical studies. Theosophy has been to me not only intellectually but also devotionally satisfying, and devotional Theosophy finds in Hindûism its most ancient and most natural expression. The student of Brahma Vidyâ may thus as a Bhakta become also Hindû, recognizing that Gnyânam and Bhakti are both necessary for the evolution of the spiritual life.

I say these few words in explanation of my own

position as Theosophist and Hindû that will be found running through these lectures, and in repudiation of the absurd story that I have been converted to Hindûism since I came to India. I became a Hindû with my full and complete acceptance of Theosophy as taught by Occultists, and there has been no change save an ever-increasing clearness of vision, an ever-expanding knowledge, and an ever-growing depth of satisfaction in the teachings embraced in 1889.

ANNIE BESANT.

Ludhiana, Feb., 1894.

The Building of the Kosmos.

I.—Sound.

THE BUILDING OF THE KOSMOS.

I.—SOUND.

BROTHERS,—When first the great Scriptures of the Hindû nation made an impression on European thought, that impression was one of a somewhat strange and remarkable character. There was a conflict amongst European thinkers as to the origin and as to the value of this ancient literature. On the one side, it was acknowledged that a profound Philosophy might there be seen; on the other, the idea of finding such a Philosophy amongst a people regarded as less civilized than those who became their critics—that idea led to much of controversy as to the way in which these books had originated, and as to the influence which had been at work in their construction. And even to-day, when the depth of their Philosophy is admitted, and the grandeur and width of their range of thought is no longer challenged, you find men like Professor Max Müller, who have given their lives to the study of these books, you find them speaking of the *Vedas* as the babblings of an infant people. You find them denying that there is any kind of secret or hidden doctrine—hidden under the veil of symbolism, concealed under the mask of allegory. It seems to me as though in the West it is impossible for thinkers to understand that you may have an infant race, and yet that race have Divine Instructors; that you may have a growing civilization, but have that civilization under the guidance of those who are specially illumined by the Spirit that is Divine. And so they have failed to understand the value of the Scriptures, seeing only the masses of the ancient people, understanding nothing of the dignity of those who stood above them as Teachers and as Guides. Trying to find what is called a purely human origin for the Scriptures, they have lamentably failed in their analysis: for where the Divine is put aside, the growth of no nation can be understood, and where the hidden Deity in man is ignored, no real grasp can be gained of Philosophy, or of Religion, or of civilization.

Now my attempt—and it must be a very imperfect attempt—in these lectures, is to vindicate the position that within the Hindû Scriptures you may find Philosophy, Science and Religion of the deepest, of the widest and of the most inspiring kind; that the Science of the West is slowly beginning to tread the paths which in these Scriptures are clearly traced; that the knowledge which the West is beginning to gather from observations of the external universe, is knowledge which may be more rapidly acquired by the study of the Scriptures, which were written by those who studied the universe from within rather than from without. Thus we may read that in the Lotus-chamber of the heart with its ether-filled space we may see everything which in the external world may be found.

> Both the heaven and earth exist within it. Both Agni and Vâyu, both the Sun and the Moon . . . and whatever else exists in this Universe[1]

are there, so that in finding his Spirit, man also finds everything which exists in the Kosmos. This is a statement not only beautiful in its poetry, but accurate in its science; and by really finding the eyes of the Spirit, those eyes that pierce through every veil of external nature, we can gain knowledge at once more accurate and more profound than can be discovered when the study is pursued purely through the eyes of the flesh.

Now in pursuing this line of investigation, very great help has been given to us by that Russian lady and great Teacher known to us as Helena Petrovna Blavatsky. Her value to the world does not lie in the question as to whether she were or were not able to perform certain acts which others might be unable to rival. Her value to the world does not lie in whether she be a wonder-worker

[1] *Chhândogyopanishad*, viii. I. 3.

or whether she be a conjurer. These points are not the points by which ultimately she will be judged by posterity. From my own standpoint these so-called marvels are matters of comparative indifference; the whole of these, while interesting from one standpoint, I look upon as of comparatively small significance. Her real value was that she unveiled to us the secret of the Ancient Knowledge, that she put into our hands the keys by which we might ourselves unlock the gates of the inner sanctuary, that she came to us knowing the things of the Spirit and able to explain to us how we for ourselves might follow the clues which she gave; so that those who are instructed in this Esoteric Philosophy—spoken of in modern times as the Theosophical Teachings—those who are instructed in it can turn to the *Vedas*, can turn to the *Purânas*, and there find knowledge which from the ordinary reader is hidden. Thus she acts as a great Teacher, filling the function which in ancient times was carried on between the Teacher and the disciple: taking the Scriptures and unfolding their inner meaning and so opening the way for spiritual progress, making it possible for us to attain to the Ancient Wisdom of the temples. I am going to try to justify that view by showing—having taken certain teachings from the ancient Hindû Scriptures—how these teachings become clearer and more easy to grasp, when they are read in the light which she has thrown upon them in the volumes spoken of by the name of *The Secret Doctrine.* I am going to support that teaching also by reference to the most advanced Science of our own day, showing you how *The Secret Doctrine,* which is really the most ancient Indian teaching, is supported on the one side in the West by what is called Science, and on the other side in the East by the Scriptures, which may be made more intelligible, more coherent, and of which the apparent contradictions vanish, when they are viewed in the light of these Secret Teachings of which a fragment only is given to the world.

Now speaking of the building of the Kosmos, I cannot at the very outset deal with the question according to Science as it is understood in Europe, because Science does not, in Europe, deal with the beginning of things. It only deals with manifestation after it has reached a certain point. It tells us nothing, as it were, of the first burgeoning out into existence of the Kosmos. It deals with nothing until we have Matter in a form which the physical senses can appreciate, or at least which the imagination, following on the lines of the physical senses, is able to construct. Tyndall has spoken of the scientific use of the imagination, and in that way we can go on scientific lines beyond that which actually may be sensated. It is no longer argued that that only is true which can be perceived by means of the senses; that was the position held some thirty years ago. It is one which the progress of Science has made it impossible to hold to-day. But you do find that Science still maintains that nothing can come within its purview save such concepts as may be formed by the intellect on the facts which have been collected by the senses; so that when you are dealing with the existence of the manifested Kosmos, you must not in your thought go beyond those material conceptions for which you already have foundation in the material phenomena that you have observed. That is, you may go beyond the aggregation of Matter that you can see, and you may posit the existence of the atom which is invisible, and which can only be seen by an effort of the scientific imagination. But you must not go beyond that which this imagination can construct out of the material supplied by the senses. Crookes, it is true, deals with the building of the atom, but even then he only carries it as far as what is called protyle or original Matter; beyond that Science will not go. It refuses to go further into the origin of things. It refuses to ask: Is it possible that behind this protyle we may still trace growth and evolution? So that in the first tracing we have only *The Secret Doctrine* and the Scriptures. We cannot bring in the scientific criticism and assistance until a little later in the argument.

Now in order that this argument may be complete from our own standpoint, I want to make a brief comparison between the beginning of things as we find it in the Shâstras, and the beginning of things as it is traced for us in the book called *The Secret Doctrine;* so that we may see, as I think we shall see, that the coherent statement that is made in the latter is exceedingly helpful, when we are puzzling ourselves somewhat over the many statements of the different aspects of the evolution that we find in the Shâstras. For you must remember that blinds have been deliberately used in these Scriptures that have been placed in our hands. We cannot, by reading them consecutively, always gain a coherent notion of the whole which in this fragment is represented, and we gain very much in time if we get a glimpse of the whole, so that when we meet the fragment, we can put it into its proper place in the edifice which we are trying to construct, instead of searching everywhere, and keeping our knowledge fragmentary, for need of that architectural plan which Madame Blavatsky really supplies.

Let us turn first to the Shâstras and see how they trace for us the origin of things. Here there is a very noticeable difference between the *Purânas* and the *Upanishads.* You will find more detail—detail given in successive descriptions, as it were—in the *Purânas;* you will find in the *Upanishads* a philosophic rather than cosmological view, especially a view which starts from the Spirit in man and shows the connection of that Spirit with the Source whence it came. This will make a difference in the view of the universe presented in these two great divisions of the Shâstras, and you will find one point especially of difference that I will put to you, which may sometimes have puzzled the reader as to the possibility of reconciliation between the two. First of all then, if I may use what seems a paradox, but is really a truth, before the "origin of things" thought is thrown backwards; for the origin of things means manifestation, it means differentiation. The very word "things" implies manifested existence. Before the manifest, there must be the One; even in European Science this is recognized, and they rightly allege the One to be inscrutable and the phenomenal to be the object of observation. But you will very rarely find that the existence of that which is behind phenomena is denied—save perhaps in some comparatively small schools of thought, that see in the universe nothing but a mass of changing phenomena, with no underlying unity in which these phenomena inhere. Generally, if Science becomes Philosophy, the One is posited as incognizable and unknowable to human thought. But there is a yet deeper conception in the Hindû view of the universe: for that which by human thought is unreachable, is still, as one may say, on the outer limit of manifestation, and even behind that outer limit, behind and beyond Brahman—who is described as invisible, intangible, unseeable, and unseizable even by thought, that which cannot be proved, and whose only proof is in the belief in the soul—behind that, there still is posited that which has no name but only a descriptive epithet, that can only be spoken of as the "beyond Brahman"—Para Brahman—of the Philosopher, the "Unmodified Vishnu" of the *Vishnu Purâna.* Now on THAT, the Unmodified Vishnu, there is nothing to be said and nothing to be thought. Neither thought nor speech has anything to do in that region, and we can only begin either to think or to speak when manifestation occurs, and when out of that darkness which may not be pierced, the first quiver comes forth which is Light, the possibility of manifested existence.

And then we come in the Scriptures to the first of all manifestations, to that which is spoken of sometimes—and notice the fact—as manifested and sometimes as unmanifested; unmanifested in itself, but manifested in the act of generation. For our thought soars, as it were, to Brahman, albeit Brahman Itself is unseizable by human thought. And we find Brahman or Its equivalent spoken of, in both those great sources of study, *Upanishads* and *Purânas*, as triple in Itself, although not triple in direct manifestation. The One, but with an inner and latent three-foldedness, which will appear gradually in manifested sequence and make the universe of things a possibility. Brahman Itself is essentially threefold; whether you take it as you may find it in the *Taittirîyopanishad*, where Brahman is spoken of as Truth, as Knowledge, as Infinity, or in that phrase which is more familiar to us, as Existence, as Bliss, as Thought. Really in these words you have the same conception—Sat-chit-ânanda—so familiar always in speaking of the Supreme, and this is but another phrase for that which you find in the *Upanishad* quoted. For what are Satyam, Gnyânam, Anantam?[1] These are only different human words which fail in the attempt to represent realities, and whether you take the one or the other threefold phrase it matters not; what you do need to grasp is that these are latent in the first Emanation, and that the beginning of the Kosmos is the unfolding of this threefold latency into manifestation, is the becoming active of the latent potentialities.

Now you have in the *Vishnu Purâna* that which represents this same thought of the triple latency; you have the first manifestation of Vishnu which is Kâla, Time, which is neither Matter nor Spirit, but which exists when both of these have disappeared into it. You may remember in the second chapter of *Vishnu Purâna* we are told that there is Pradhâna, which is the essence of Matter, Purusha, which is the essence of Spirit; when these disappear, the form of Vishnu that is Time remains; thus there is this conception of Time without beginning and without ending, which, as it were, stands behind the next manifestations, joins them, and makes them possible. Then you come to the

1 *Taittirîyopanishad*, Brahmânanda Vallî, First Anuvâka.

second stage, which in this *Purâna* is given under the name of Pradhâna-Purusha, essential Matter, essential Spirit—out of the One, the Two, which means manifestation; and that is why Brahman is spoken of as both unmanifest and manifest. It is unmanifest in Itself; It is manifest when the Two appear from the One, and this duality makes the Kosmos possible. Then you may find many words in many books, all of which convey the same thought: the duality on which so much stress has been laid by Subba Rao—whose death every Philosopher must regret for the work that he might have done in this unification of the secret and the published thought. You have Mûlaprakriti and Daiviprakriti —which are only other expressions for that which in Greek thought is called the Logos—in manifestation. Again, you have the one characteristic given you of that Pradhâna, that it is Vyaya, extensible; you cannot begin to describe, because attributes are not yet evolved, but you have the one characteristic of extensibility, which always means the possibility of form; so that in this Second, which is manifested from the One, there is the essence of form—that which is to take on manifold appearances—and you have also that which is to come out in form, the Purusha which moulds, working on the Pradhâna, and thereby makes the manifoldness of the manifested universe possible. Then there is—still following the *Vishnu Purâna* —the third stage, or Mahat, that which is to be the controlling and directing force, that which is to be the Over-ruler, as we may say, which in every case will guide the evolution of the universe, and make it consistent, reasonable, right through; and here I cannot but remind you for a moment that, in the last expression, I have used a thought which we lately heard from Professor Huxley. He speaks of an Intelligence that "pervades the universe,"[1] recognizing, as it were, such an Intelligence after professing Agnosticism for so many years. There is an Intelligence of which he is obliged to admit the pervading quality, which is essentially the same as that fundamental conception of Mahat, which is intelligence without limitation, save such limitation as the very fact of manifestation must imply.

Now these three stages in this clear, definite presentment from the *Vishnu Purâna* are somewhat difficult to trace in the *Upanishads*, but let me say before leaving their presentation in the *Purâna* that the Three are but the unfoldment of the One, of the Satchitânanda which you have latent in the First. You have differentiated Them when you regard Them as three. The First is then Sat, pure Existence. What is the Second, which is dual, save Ânanda, for the very fact of bliss implies duality? What is Mahat but Chit in manifestation? So that it is really a process of unfolding, as I said; all that which is latent in the One becoming manifest in the Three. In the *Upanishads*

[1] *Evolution and Ethics*, p. 35.

this unfolding is somewhat veiled. There is a tendency in the *Upanishads* to pass directly from the Brahman in which all is latent, to the Spirit in man which is Brahman in the heart—the Logos of the individual Soul. None the less in the *Upanishads* here and there you will find traces given which show you that the same thought is present which is more definitely unfolded in Paurânic writings. You will find if you will turn to the *Mundakopanishad*, it is said there that from Brahman is produced Life—which is Ânanda—and Mind, which is Chit; then it goes on to the five elements, ether, air, light and the rest.[1] So that you do have the same succession, although but little stress is laid upon it, the object of the writer being different from the unfolding of the Kosmos. So again you may find in the *Brihadâranyakopanishad* the trinity of Life, Name and Form. Life, from which the Two proceed; and Life is concealed by Name and Form, that is, the First is concealed by Its dual manifestation. So also you will find the same idea in the *Kathopanishad* in the succession which is traced in the gradual search after Spirit; when you have gone through Manas to Buddhi, from Buddhi to Âtmâ, beyond Âtmâ there is the Unmanifested, and beyond the Unmanifested there is the Great Soul, therein spoken of as Purusha. Thus you get this most suggestive fact, that between the Spirit in man, and that beyond which there is naught, there

[1] *Mundaka*, ii. I. 3.

is given but one stage, "the Unmanifested." What is the underlying thought of that single instead of triple presentation? It is to tell those whose eyes are opened that to the Spirit in man there is but One between it and That which is unknowable, for the Logos of the Soul is one, and one is the Ray of which the Spirit is the reflection in the heart; so that in the *Upanishad*, which is meant to lead you to the finding of the unity of the Spirit with its Lord, everything is ignored save that one Logos to which the Spirit belongs, and the very Kosmos in its multiplicity disappears when the Spirit itself is seeking the source whence it came.

Now turning from this sketch taken from the Scriptures themselves, let us take *The Secret Doctrine*—I am using that name simply for the book called by it—we shall find that the whole of these most complicated teachings are presented in a form so simple, so clear, that we may take it as a clue to guide us in studying the far more difficult form in which it is presented to us in the Hindû writings. It being built entirely on the same foundation as that of the Shâstras, you find first postulated Para Brahman, on Which nothing may be said: and then the presentment of the three Logoi,—the word Logos being used, as being more familiar in Western thought, and as having—as we shall see in a moment when I come to deal with Sound—special significance with regard to the building of the Kosmos. The very word Logos implies the Builder, inasmuch as the uttered sound is the Great Builder of all manifested forms. And then we have traced for us the succession of these three Logoi, only the ancient Trimûrti under another name, that we have been studying in the Scriptures themselves; we have the First Logos unmanifest, that is one title which is given to it. The First, the Unmanifest, appears but to disappear, because so far as Kosmos is concerned, the First Logos is unmanifested; it can only become manifest to the Spirit in man which is one with Itself. Then the One differentiated into Two, and, using the language of the West, this duality is described as "Spirit-Matter"—not Spirit *and* Matter, for you have but two aspects of the One, and if you divide them in thought you begin with a mistaken conception. The universe does not grow out of Spirit and Matter—two separate conceptions—it is an evolution from Spirit-Matter, or the One with a dual aspect. And so in this second you have, as I said, the Ânanda aspect, and you find H. P. Blavatsky laying great stress on this fundamental unity which yet becomes dual in manifestation, Spirit-Matter, Purusha-Pradhâna. These are but the two primeval aspects of the One and the Secondless. And then when she went on to throw to the careful student a hint as to the symbolism of the subject, by which he may unveil this fundamental mystery of the Kosmos, you find her dealing with the symbolism of the moon and suddenly throwing into the paragraph on the moon this phrase:

> Lunar magnetism generates life, preserves and destroys it; and Soma embodies the triple power of the Trimûrti, though it passes unrecognized by the profane.[1]

Then a little further on she speaks of

> The One Divine Essence, *unmanifested*, perpetually begetting a Second Self, *manifested*, which Second Self, androgynous in its nature, gives birth *in an immaculate way* to every thing macro- and micro-cosmical in this Universe.

In this sentence in which the writer throws in the notion of the moon in an apparently somewhat curious way, you have the key to much of the allegory which will explain to you these obscure beginnings of the building of the Kosmos. From one side you have the sun and from the other side the moon. On the one side you have the light, and on the other side the water; fire and water everywhere, as that by which the building of the universe may take place, and fire and water are but the names for Spirit and Matter, and but express this duality of the Second Logos. In this second manifestation fire is the Daiviprakriti or the Light of the Logos; water is a manifestation of the Mûlaprakriti or the root of all Matter. As they proceed, it is along this dual line; and the moon (as is known by every student) is constantly represented as androgynous, sometimes as male, sometimes as female, to-day as God, King Soma, to-

[1] *The Secret Doctrine*, i. 398; *n.e.* pp. 427, 428.

morrow as Goddess, so that this is always pressed on your attention. When you think of the moon you have the double side, positive and negative, that which in our world we recognize as sex. Thus we have perpetually this antithetical duality, without which no building can be, for you must have the passive which nourishes the universe, you must have the active which fecundates; otherwise there is no possibility of reproduction, there is no existence for the universe manifest at all. And then the Third is Mahat, the same name for the ideating power, thought, intellect, which is to be at the very root of existence. So that here again life and thought are to be primary; wherever you find an atom of manifested existence, you will find in it this duality, which it takes from its source; for out of the dual the dual must proceed, and you will neither have unliving Matter nor senseless Energy. Such existences are impossible in a universe that has been generated by Life and by Thought. And this Trinity is, in the deepest sense, of sevenfold constitution, for in the three lie enfolded the seven, as also in the Trimûrti, when you begin to think, you will find the seven involved; for in the Trimûrti you are obliged to recognize in each the Shakti side, or duality in each, so that your three must become six; wherever you realize the One you are obliged in manifestation to realize the Two; you cannot have Vishnu without Lakshmî, you cannot have Shiva without Durga, the two are always recognizable, so that when you think of the Trimûrti you are really thinking of six, and the Seventh is that which synthesizes all, and without which this differentiation could never appear; so that in the very foundation of the Kosmos the septenary appears, and it is only the lack of insight in us which has blinded us to that so long. When we reach this stage, the stage of Mahat, or intelligence, at once we come to the possibility of the manifestation in which Western Science also may play its part; from the word Mahat, you have the threefold Ahamkâra, which essentially has the qualities so familiar to every student of the Gîtâ, so familiar to every student I may say of Philosophy as a whole—the true or pure, the active or brilliant, the dark or elemental—that Matter of threefold quality which is necessary for further manifestation, and in which we shall find manifoldness will appear. So we learn, if we take the *Vishnu Purâna*, that from the Tâmasic quality proceed the elements—not the elements of which Western Science speaks, but the five ancient elements; we have no good English equivalent for Bhutâdi. It is from Ahamkâra that the material universe proceeds; first it generates Âkâsha, from Âkâsha air, from air fire, from fire water, and from water earth. Now why this succession? First Âkâsha: of that we are told the characteristic is Sound; the rudiment of Sound is evolved, and that is the only attribute of Âkâsha. Then air, and what is air in this sense? Certainly not the air of the atmosphere, certainly not that which is the air of later manifestation, a mingling of gases where the atom has already appeared. The great "Air" of the *Upanishads* and of the *Purânas* is the breath of the Supreme, essentially Motion, for only when this conception of motion comes in, is any manifestation possible. So that first you have the Âkâsha, whose only attribute is Sound; then you have the Motion which is given to that Âkâsha by the great Breath; and in these you have sound, and then touch, which is the second sense, and from sound and touch—your very Âkâsha and Air—you have Fire generated, for which this friction between Breath and Âkâsha is necessary, and that is the Electricity, without which no further growth can be, and not until you have this succession of Âkâsha, which can take form from Breath, which can give form to Electricity, which can build into aggregation, until this there does not become possible atomic constitution, from which you may have your water and earth, or the liquid and solid manifestations of that which hitherto has been the so-called "immaterial." And notice how that succession is, as it were, guaranteed to us intellectually by the senses of man; see how the first is correlated with the sense of hearing, how the second with both sound and touch, the second sense; how with the fire there comes light which is correlated with vision, so that then you have sound and touch and vision; how then there comes water which is correlated with taste, because without moisture taste cannot be, and the four are present; and, lastly, earth, whose essential characteristic is smell, the last of the senses to be evolved in the physical, and therefore the first of the senses to be found on the astral plane when the soul is passing backwards to seek itself. H. P. Blavatsky, of course following this, has already pointed out that the Âkâsha is that which is generated from the Third Logos, and that its only characteristic is Sound. But here at once comes in our Modern Science, and in this conception of the Âkâsha in which is working the great Breath, so that by the Âkâsha and Vâyu Agni may appear, we find ourselves face to face with the very latest theories and discoveries of Science, and with that genesis of the elements—which is only another term for the building of the Kosmos—which you may study in Western language in the writings of Mr. Crookes. Madame Blavatsky in the first volume of *The Secret Doctrine* wrote to a considerable extent on these discoveries of Crookes so far as they had been published when that book was written; but she pointed out that there were some points which still were lacking. And it is noticeable that only just at the end of her life—it was in 1891, only a couple of months before her death—Mr. Crookes, speaking before an audience of the picked Scientists of England, stated that that which had been a hypothesis, had become a certainty, and that he was now able to put forward as definitely ascertained theories, things which before he had only been able to suggest as hypotheses which might be useful as a guide to discovery. And what is this great discovery of his which it was said by one of those who listened to him would put his name on a level with the greatest thinkers and the greatest Scientists of our time? It was the discovery that the atom was not eternal, that the atom was produced and not primary, that it was destructible, and therefore had come into existence—for only that which is indestructible is eternal, as every Philosophy will admit. And he showed that the atom must be looked upon as dual, that it must be regarded as a neutral body formed by the joining of the positive and negative elements in Nature, and that the atom was permanent just because of its duality, because as it were the two were knit together, and that gave it its stability and its power to act as the brick, so to speak, in the building of the world; and then behind the atom he placed what he called "the protyle," borrowing the name from an Occultist of mediæval Europe, Roger Bacon, who had used the same word to denote the primeval substance. When he wanted to trace how these atoms were builded, then he found himself compelled to posit protyle as primeval substance. Note how the professor closely followed on the line of ancient thought, when he found himself obliged to posit Motion—that is, the great Breath, which is the second element after Âkâsha, without which the Âkâsha would remain motionless and therefore without generating anything. Having protyle and motion, he then posits the third, that is the force allied to electricity, which he says traces for itself a spiral course through the space filled with matter. As this spiral course is traced, atom after atom is generated by the aggregation of the protyle; and so all these atoms are formed, falling into definite chemical classes according to the position that they hold in the spiral which is traced by the electrical force. And the spiral is a necessary form: why? First you have motion; imagine the motion is in one direction. As that motion in one direction proceeds through homogeneous matter, it compresses the matter together; and as the matter solidifies, it loses heat. It is a familiar fact that such a fall of temperature must occur; it is one of the most familiar experiments in elementary chemistry, that where matter passes from one state to another, from gas to liquid, from liquid to solid, or from solid to liquid, liquid to gas, that according to the process of the change heat is either given out or else becomes latent. To take the common illustration, if ice becomes water, heat becomes latent to an extent of what is called 80 units, before there is any change in the outer appearance or temperature of the ice. So when the temperature changes with the solidifying of the elements, what must be the result? The result must be that the line representing the motion must change its direction; and with the fall of temperature there will be a change in motion; if you want to represent it, you must no longer have the straightforward line, but one which is the resultant of two combined forces moving in different directions, therefore the necessary tracing of a spiral; so that the ancient symbol of the Serpent, so familiar in our literature—the Serpent of which I shall have something to say to-morrow—is the most significant symbol of the spiral coiling itself continually, and it thus gives us the very picture of the Kosmic Motion. It is that which our great Scientists were obliged to make when generalizing force in the Kosmos, and the genesis of the elements comes about by this spiral or serpentine motion. This motion H. P. Blavatsky calls the spiral motion of Fohat in Space, for Fohat underlies all forces, and by it the force of electricity is generated.

With this there comes Sound. You cannot have Motion in Matter without generating vibration; and all vibration is fundamentally Sound; all vibration is changeable into Sound, transmutable into Sound; and the old phrase that the Serpent glides hissing through Space carries with it a very real signification. Therefore is it that the first property generated in Âkâsha is Sound—the Word, the Logos; and you may remember there again how Subba Rao has put this very plainly and very beautifully when he is speaking of the uttered Sound, of the uttered Word, where he speaks of Fohat as instrument of the Word, and where he points out to us that that which we utter is the Vaikarî Vâch—that is "the whole Kosmos in its objective form";[1] for the whole Universe is but the uttering of the Word which is latent in the unmanifested Logos, and which is spoken in the second Logos; it is this spoken Word which is the objective Kosmos. So alike in Kosmos and in man is this power of Sound—Sound without which form cannot be, Sound which is the builder of form, which generates form, every Sound having its own form, and every Sound being of this triple character, that it generates form, that it upholds form, that it destroys form. Thus, once again, the Trimûrti appears, the Creator, the Preserver, the Destroyer; they are all One in different aspects, for the Divine is One, whatever the form of Its manifestation. And here indeed may we bring together ancient and modern thought; Shabda Brahman is the force that builds the Kosmos, but it is also the force by which a Yogî brings about all the powers within himself; and so, as I say, taking our Western Science, we can now bring, in support of this form-building power of Sound, a number of what are called facts, which to some persons are more convincing than those deeper realities of which the fact is only the phenomenal expression. These facts which Modern

[1] See *The Secret Doctrine*, i. 138; *n.e.* p. 162.

Science has gathered with respect to Sound, are valuable to us, not as teaching us—they ought not to have anything to teach us—but as enabling us to convince others who have not understood the value of the Scriptures, though the Scriptures give the essence of which Science only gives the outer manifestation. What then are some of those facts which substantiate the position of the ancient writers that Sound lies at the very origin of forms, and that the multiplicity of forms simply depends upon the variety of the sounds. First, we shall find one of the earliest experiments with regard to Sound—one of the clumsiest, although at the time it seemed beautiful enough. Take, for instance, an ordinary drum, so that in the parchment head of this drum you have a vibrating surface. If you take the bow with which you throw the strings of a violin into vibration, and draw this bow across the edge of the parchment, then a note is given out—a note which depends of course on the tension in the parchment and various other matters which are not important to us. That is simple enough; but it was thought desirable to try to discover what happened when the note was given out; and in order that that which is invisible might be made visible, sand was lightly scattered over the surface of the drum; then the bow was drawn across the edge of the circle of the drum, and this experiment was done over and over again at every point in this circle which was the circumference of the drum. Let me say in passing that European Science is admirable in its patience, in the way in which it repeats over and over again until it gets the fact; in that it is worthy of our admiration, for in that fashion only can these phenomenal facts be discovered. In every portion of the circumference that was experimented upon, it was found that as the bow was drawn across, the sand was thrown up in the air, but it was also found that when it came back it did not fall evenly over the surface, but formed a geometrical figure. So that the sand spread over the parchment was by sound compelled to assume definite geometrical shapes, different as the notes were changed in character by bowing different points in the circumference. As different intervals in the circumference gave out different harmonics of the fundamental note, it was found different shapes were produced; that at first, touching it at a particular point, you will only get the drum divided into four, because that is the fundamental note given out by the parchment vibrating as a whole. When you make it vibrate in harmonics you have geometrical shapes of a far more elaborate character. And following out these investigations of harmonics—as they were called—we discover that in every note that is sounded, you have not got a single sound but a very complex sound that can be divided and subdivided. What seems to us simple is complex; when you strike a note you are sounding a large number of notes at the same time, and the highly trained ear can discover such harmonics; it is the difference of harmonics that gives difference of quality to the sound. Now it is found that the difference of quality, or this splitting-up of one sound into many, was shown to the eyes by the shapes that were traced by this falling of the sand. They then began to get out this difference in a more delicate way, for the sand was a heavy substance, and this parchment was rather a clumsy vibrating material, so that they got more delicate substances, and lighter and lighter finely-divided stuff, such as delicate seeds or the spores of the Lycopodium. This is one of the best things to experiment with, because it is so very light that a very fine vibration throws it into forms. Then they tried tuning-forks—steel forks which, vibrating, give different notes. They obtained the vibrations by means of mirrors arranged to throw a traced picture of the vibrations by the magic lantern through a magnifying lens on to a sheet; and in this way the invisible vibrations of the tuning-fork were traced and magnified and were there seen to form beautiful geometrical designs. On the sheet on which the image from the magic lantern was thrown, it was found that every note gave rise to exquisite forms, which were changed as the note was changed, so that really whenever you are playing any piece of music you are forming the most exquisite shapes in the ether and the air around. That is the way in which pulses of sound are in these ingenious fashions made visible to the eye by throwing them from the magic lantern on to the screen; so that the invisible was made visible, and the power of Sound was made manifest to the eye as well as to the ear.

Still further investigations were made, and Mrs. Watts-Hughes proved that when notes were sung into a horn-shaped instrument and a succession of notes thus sounded, more elaborate forms could be builded, forms such as ferns, trees, and flowers—all these were generated by the notes of the human voice. In order still further to analyze and see how this was done, a clever instrument was invented, in which two pendulums were set swinging, each of the pendulums having its own motion. These pendulums were made to interact with each other, and the motion of one pendulum modified the motion of the other; from these pendulums with their interacting motions, with a pencil attached by means of a lever which could be moved in the resultant direction obtained from the two pendulums, most elaborate forms were traced on a card put under the point of the pencil, so that successive motions might be observed; and most marvellously complicated forms were thus obtained, forms like shells of the most elaborate description, geometrical shapes perfect in their angles and perfect in their curves. Now as the vibrations of a note are always in one direction, and as the pendulum motions were simply swinging backwards and forwards, the interferences of the pendulums, which were made to modify each other, were really the reproduction of the true vibrations interfering with each other or modifying each other. Thus was obtained a graphic picture of the modifications which might be caused by vibrations which were interfering, although each separate one was in one direction; and you find that the result of the interference was this marvellous elaboration of form; and just similarly to that, you find that the result of the interference of the light-waves is colour. Wherever you break up light-waves and thus make one interfere with another, you get colour coming forth and manifesting itself; so that what we call colour in mother-of-pearl is only the result of a very delicate roughness in the surface which makes interference of the light vibrations with each other; by these pendulums were shown the interference of the vibrations of Sound. So Science has shown us how forms are builded by Sound, and looking at the outside of Nature, we are struck by the strange fact that everywhere we find geometrical shapes. Take the crystal which is found in the mineral world. Every crystal is builded along certain axes of direction. Every crystal takes its shape from these axes of direction. The simplest crystals are built on the simplest lines, and the more elaborate the crystal the more numerous will be the axes which have their centre in the middle of the crystal. Each crystal is built along these axes, and the difference of the crystals depends upon this fundamental arrangement of the axes; so that in the building of the crystals in the mineral world geometrical shapes appear once more. But you cannot separate the crystal from the crystalloid. The crystalloid is like the form of the crystal in the mineral world, but it is found in the vegetable world. No longer is the mineral in Nature divided from the vegetable world, but in the vegetables these bodies are formed of a different kind of material and they are not called crystals but crystalloids. Here again these axes appear and the same suggestion of geometrical form on which the vegetable world is to be built. When we study the vegetable world we go still further. Take for instance a twig of a tree; note and study the arrangement of the leaves on it. You will find that the leaves are arranged in a spiral. The spiral, coming forth once more as the generating force, directs the arrangement of the leaves; sometimes very simple, sometimes very complicated. Take a very simple case like that of the apple tree—which is very familiar to us in England—where the spiral is what we call $\frac{2}{5}$; in this the spiral has a double turn, and there are five leaves, which are placed on the points, so to speak, of the spiral, until you have to begin again when five are complete. You will find, if you take a bit of string and twist it twice round the stem or twig of the tree, that on this spiral you have touched five leaves which are arranged at equal intervals on the string. If you take another kind of plant you will find a different arrangement, but still the spiral; another plant will have another and different arrangement, but still the spiral; so that when the plant is sending out its leaves, it is always working under this law of spiral arrangement, and there is this geometrical rule which governs the apparently irregular sending forth of leaves and flowers. There is no irregularity; the most apparently irregular arrangement is only a complicated series of interlacing spirals; for sometimes instead of one spiral you have two; in a few cases you have three spirals, and these three by going round the stem, interlacing, make extremely complicated arrangements which look like confusion; but "that which is Chaos to the senses is Kosmos to the reason." You will always find this geometrical arrangement underneath the apparently chaotic heaps which you may observe by the eye or the senses. Is it not true as Plato said, that "God geometrizes"? Is not this the fundamental conception of the Scriptures, that Sound-vibration is the builder of form? Is that not justified by these discoveries of Modern Science?

Not only can Sound build; Sound can also destroy. Strange that the same force should produce opposite results. People have laughed at it, when it is said in Religion. They are obliged to admit it, when Science repeats what Religion so long has said. That which in Religion is incredible contradiction, in Science has to be reconciled by the discovery of the unifying truth. Why cannot we apply the same theory in Religion when we find what seems to be contradiction? Why cannot we study and seek for that underlying truth, which will make the apparent contradictions but aspects, as the two sides of one shield? Thus the builder of form destroys it; and whereas gentle vibrations build, vehement vibrations tear apart that which the gentle ones have brought together. Inasmuch as no form is solid, but every form consists of molecules with spaces between them, the vibration of the Sound going between the molecules makes them vibrate more and more strongly, throws them further and further apart, until the time comes when the attracting force which keeps them together being overcome, they shoot out and the form becomes disintegrated.

If you take a glass, and you discover its fundamental note—as you may very easily do by half filling it up with water, and drawing a bow across it, and seeing how the water is divided—when you discover the fundamental note, produce that note on some instrument from which you are able to obtain great intensity and loudness of sound; then your glass first will give out the note and you can hear it coming from the glass; you will see the water in the glass thrown into vibration though no one has touched it. The sound grows louder, and the wavelets of the water that show you how it is acting get bigger and bigger, become more and more turbulent, until dashing against each other they make wave tumults instead of harmony, and then the vibrations of the molecules of the glass which cause all these movements in the water become too great for the glass to stand them; it shivers in every direction. So again Tyndall has taken a glass rod, and rubbing it gently has produced a sound; but making that sound intense, the rod has shivered and disappeared: there were only circular fragments of the glass rod, showing the power of the note which the glass itself had generated. So that everywhere we have the proof that Sound can disintegrate form and can create form; as you see, Sound may act either as builder or preserver or destroyer; for preserver I say it is, since without Sound nothing exists. Everything is in constant motion; one sort of motion builds the form, another preserves the form, a third destroys the form; and the destruction of one form is only the building of another. That which is destroyer in one shape is creator in another. There is no annihilation; for every death in one sphere is a birth into another. So let us finish this rough sketch of this part of the building of the Kosmos and of the power of Sound, by showing how it justifies what has been called superstition and folly, and the mere bablings of an ignorant people with regard to the uses of Sound! As long as there has been a Hindû faith, the power of Sound has been recognized in the sacred Word; in that Word lie all potencies; for the sacred Word expresses the One and only Being, every power of generation, of preservation and of destruction. Therefore has been forbidden the careless use of that Word; therefore forbidden its use amongst mixed audiences; therefore should it never be sounded where many people are gathered together, and where mingling and hostile magnetisms are making a confused atmosphere, so that any great sound thrown into it must cause tumult and not harmony; therefore was it never to be sounded save when the mind was pure; never to be sounded save when the mind was tranquil; never to be used save where the life was noble; because the sound that working in the harmonious builds, working in the inharmonious destroys; and everything that is evil is tumultuous, while everything which is pure is harmonious. For the great Breath, which is purity, goes forth in rhythmical vibration, and all that is one with that rhythm is essentially pure and therefore harmonious. But when the great Breath, working on Matter, finds friction, then it is that impurity is set up, and if man in his own atmosphere—using that breath which comes out from him, which is the reflection of the Supreme Breath—is impure, that is, inharmonious, then to sound the name of the Supreme under these circumstances is to invite his own destruction, his own disintegration, for he throws the very force of the Divine into disharmony. What then can he do but destroy that which has nothing in common with the divine harmony? And this is true not only of the sacred Word, but of the mantra that is used to build. Why is it—have you ever thought of it—that when a new life is to be builded within the womb of the mother, mantras are repeated? Why? In order that their building forces may work on the growing life and that it may be thrown into harmonious vibrations, so that that which shall be born may be worthy to be the habitation of a noble Soul. Why is it that from the moment of conception, religion begins for the Hindû? It is because the Spirit must never be without Religion, because, when the Spirit is coming towards its human birth, it is necessary that these forces of Religion should surround it, and help in the building of its earthly home. And so also with sacred Sound the new-born life is welcomed in its very incoming into this world of manifestation; that the sacred harmony may surround it, and give it the impulse in the birth hour, which shall send it on towards harmonious development. Step by step this harmony is to mould the growing life, and when the time comes that the Spirit can work more directly on the physical body, you mark it by the ceremony of initiation which gives to the child the mantra which is to be the key-note of the future life. Therefore the mantra should come from one who knows the key-note of that life, and is able to give it the sounds which are wanted to keep it harmonious right through life. Here comes in this great preserving power of Sound; so that whenever that life is in danger this Sound may protect; whenever that life is threatened by visible or invisible menace, that murmur of the muttered mantra may come between it and the danger, making around it waves of harmony, from which every evil thing shall be thrown back by the force of the vibrations. Let any foe come against it, that foe is flung backwards when it touches these vibrations. And so onwards again right through life to the death hour. Every morning through life that chanted mantram shall give the key-note to the day, and the whole day shall be made harmonious and be brought into rhythm with the sound with which the day has begun; and when the day closes and the sun is sinking once more, the chant should be resounded, so that the disharmony of the day may be rendered harmonious, and the Spirit may be made fit to go onwards in the night time towards its Lord. And when the death hour has come and the Spirit must pass onwards into other regions of the universe, the chanted mantram accompanies it. In the ceremonies of Shrâddha there are used special sounds which shall break the bondage-house of the Soul, and which shall destroy the body generated on the other side of death which keeps the Soul in prison. So to the very threshold of Devaloka, Sound accompanies it, until it passes into that Loka where the chants of the Devas shall ever surround it in its sojourning with an ocean of harmony, which is not mingled with the discord of the earth; shall there keep it in perfect rest and perfect bliss till the word comes to go backward to the earth, in order that it may serve as harmonizer of Nature once again.

The Building of the Kosmos.

II.—Fire.

THE BUILDING OF THE KOSMOS.

II.—FIRE.

MY BROTHERS,—We saw yesterday, in dealing with the building of the Kosmos, that the great Breath was the moving agent, and that that Breath gave to the Âkâsha its property of Sound, its primary characteristic. Now looking at things either from the standpoint of Eastern knowledge or from that of modern Western investigation, we find that the differences between what are called the reports of the senses are differences in the translation by the consciousness of outside impulses, those impulses being fundamentally the same. The result of the great Breath, throwing the Âkâsha into action, may be translated in different ways, when it reaches our consciousness, according to the fashion in which we sensate it. So that it is true to say either from the Eastern or from the Western standpoint that sensations differ according to the organ that receives them, the differences being caused by the body through which the sensations are received, the consciousness translating into different tones that which fundamentally is the same. So, in studying Western Science you will learn that all senses belonging to the body are developed from a primary sense, and that the primary sense is that which is called the sense of touch.

There has lately been much investigation into the nature and action of ether, which is the lowest form of what we know as Âkâsha. For Âkâsha is the primary substance of which ether is one of the lower manifestations in connection with our own solar system. That substance has Motion, as we saw yesterday; but the Air is the great Breath in the Âkâsha, and it is that which gives rise to this feeling of touch. We saw Sound was evolved, with which hearing is correlated, and then we have touch, correlated with Vâyu, as the great Breath. All these vibrations in the ether, from the standpoint of Modern Science, are but modes, as they are called, of motion; and the reception of the mode of motion by the individual decides the name which shall be given to it. Thus Modern Science teaches that Sound is one mode of motion in which air takes part. Light is another mode of motion, purely ethereal, it is said. Lately electricity has been recognized as another mode of motion. Heat is another mode of motion, and so on. Thus there has gradually appeared in Western Science that sense of unity which has always characterized knowledge in the East; so that everything which in the phenomenal has a different appearance assumes to the consciousness this fundamental unity. Therefore in dealing with Light we are only dealing with another aspect in consciousness of primary motion, and that which from one aspect to us is Sound, in another aspect to us is Light. Therefore it will be reasonable to expect, as we shall indeed find, that the same fundamental conceptions are expressed at one time as Sound and at another time as Light, and that everywhere in the Kosmos, sound and colour are interchangeable, as I shall show you that they have been proved to be phenomenally interchangeable by some of the latest experiments which have been carried on in the West. Taking then the vibration known as Light as that which is to occupy our thought this morning, that Light would be the synonym in all the ancient books for THAT which is beyond conception, THAT which we spoke of yesterday as only to be expressed—if I may use again an inaccurate phrase—by the descriptive phrase Para Brahman, or beyond Brahman. "Darkness" is the word which in the Scriptures is always used to convey to us this primary thought—Darkness infinite and complete; which expresses nothing, for it is beyond the possibility of expression; which conveys no idea, because idea is limitation and implies separation of that which is thought from that which is not thought, and in this there can be no separation; there is no thought, because thought means that difference has appeared; and therefore Darkness, in which there is neither the visible nor the invisible, is the best symbol—Darkness, absolute, eternal, incomprehensible; it is that which is behind every manifestation of Light, as of everything else which we can put into human language. And from the Darkness first is Light—but Light formless; visible indeed, as coming into manifestation, but without form, for form would imply still something beyond it; space which has no form. So that Brahman is described as "luminous without form," the pure idea of Light, an idea which needs, of course, that use of the imagination which we spoke of, because to us it is always the light-giving body of which we conceive; whereas here you must not conceive of a body, you must not conceive of a form, you must think of Light divorced from everything which would limit it, and therefore "luminous without form"—as you will find Brahman spoken of in the *Mundakopanishad*.[1] That, then, will be the first idea: Darkness, and from that, Light.

And, strangely enough, in this conception of things Modern Science has also a word to say; for taking the conception of Motion with which we have connected the great Breath, darkness is consistent with motion from the standpoint of human consciousness. Light is indeed a form of motion, but vibration, which is too rapid or too slow to give

[1] *Mundaka*, ii. I. 2.

light, gives us darkness—a most significant fact, if for a moment you let it rest in the mind that where you think of vibrations so rapid that they cannot be sensed by the eye, there darkness is the answer of consciousness to this exceedingly rapid vibration. In truth, beyond human consciousness as now existing, there is possibility—and we cannot say that there may not be endless possibilities—of existence beyond that which our senses can sensate. Thus Science tells us that vibrations so intensely rapid that the eye cannot answer to them will be translated to the consciousness as darkness, and only with the slackening of the vibration will there be light. Now translate that scientific thought into metaphysical language, and you have the very coming into manifestation of the universe; for as that which is beyond thought slackens itself for manifestation, then it becomes manifested as Light. And so even in the visible universe you will find that we have that which is truly in its essence light, but which shows no light—because the waves are too rapid; and we have to slacken those rapid vibrations by throwing them through a particular preparation, if we desire that luminosity should appear. So that when the universe is to become manifested and substance is to evolve, as it were, there is slackening of the Motion in the Infinite Darkness, and with the slackening of its vibrations Light without form appears. It seems as though we have had from the West a suggestion of the depth of this ancient Eastern thought, and as though Western thought in its experimental fashion were groping towards the very idea which we find at the beginning of things in the Eastern books.

From this radiance, which is without form, from this luminosity, which is Light in its essence manifesting itself—it is sometimes called "cold Flame" so as to exclude even the notion of heat from this pure Light—we have that second manifestation, the Second Logos which we spoke of yesterday, and then the Light becomes Fire. No longer absolutely formless, no longer without heat; but with the further slackening of the Light, as manifestation proceeds, there will be generated heat, and you will then have Fire, of which the essence is heat, and the cold, formless Flame will become the Fire which is the active agent in the building of the Kosmos. But Fire cannot appear alone, its very nature implying as it does something more than the Light whence it springs, implying that by friction heat must come into existence; also it involves the further conception of that duality which we spoke of yesterday when we were dealing with the dual manifestation under Sound; and so when we have Fire, we cannot think of it without its action, and always the first action of Fire is the development of moisture. So that in this Second Logos or manifestation in the dual form, Fire and Water are the two things that come to us in thought; Fire which is Spirit in its essence, Water which is always the symbol for the essence of Matter; and just as we found Spirit-Matter the Second Logos, and found there the very origin of the possibility of Sound, so looking at it from the standpoint of Light, we have this conception of Fire and Water, of the Light of the Logos and that in which it works. Of this the Lotus has ever been the symbol, growing out of the navel of Vishnu, hidden beneath the waters from which life is to spring; for that Vishnu, who is not floating on the waters but is concealed beneath them, is in this aspect the First Logos, and the Lotus that grows upward from his navel is the Second Logos, and is the symbol of Fire and Water; for in the Lotus leaves, rising to a point, you have the upward-springing flames, and they float on the water. And the Lotus has been ever held as the symbol of Creative Fire, in the womb of which is to be generated heat, the active creative force. Therefore within the Lotus blossom, or the Lotus bud as it is at first, there is the Third Logos, Brahmâ, or the active creative agency, which is synonymous with Mahat, or the creative intelligence in the womb of the Fire; and as the Fire opens out then there comes the second form of Flame which is creative, not the cold Flame of the First Logos, but the burning Flame of the Third, which from the Sea of Fire is to build up the Kosmos, and make the universe possible.

And when we turn to the light that has been

thrown on this ancient and not difficult conception for those who have carefully studied—when we turn to the writings of Madame Blavatsky, we shall find that this is very clearly put; so that taking these as a clue, we are able to unravel the symbolism to which we have just now referred. For Fire she uses ether in its purest form, the substance of ether, before we can speak of it as Âkâsha. And there are two Fires, and a distinction is made between them in the Occult teaching; the first, purely formless and invisible, is concealed in the Central Spiritual Sun, and is spoken of as triple, metaphysically. There again we have the triple nature of the Logos in which these Fires body themselves forth, and then the Fire manifesting as Kosmos which is to be septenary, both throughout the universe and our solar system; exactly the same as we found yesterday, where we had the triple unfolding itself into seven. And here we have the formless Flame —the cold Flame or Light—the Fire, and then the Heat or the creative Flame, the same symbolism under another aspect, the same essential idea given in another form. Therefore always have we learnt that the Light of the Logos, Daiviprakriti, or the brilliant side of Substance, has been the generative and creative agent; and you must remember that dealing with the symbolic Lotus that I alluded to, you have heard of it as hermaphrodite, bringing back the same idea of duality into our thought, that yesterday we found as the characteristic of the

Second Logos or the second manifested energy which is to build the universe. From this you get that force which in its lower forms is electricity, magnetism, and heat; but another kind of motion still, but another action of the great Breath, and it is that which in Theosophical literature is so often spoken of as Fohat—rightly translated by Subba Rao as the Light of the Logos; for it is the energizing agent, it is that which, springing forth, has to build the Kosmos, that Fiery Serpent which is the creative agency. You must remember how I yesterday spoke of this, and how I alluded to it in the latest discoveries of Mr. Crookes as symbolizing electricity, and the way in which the spiral form was produced owing to the fall in temperature; here we see it as the Fiery Serpent, and as the Fiery Dragon in the milky ocean breathing forth Fire, and so building all forms of manifestation. Wherever you see the Serpent of Fire, wherever you see it becoming a circle with the tail in its mouth, then it is that you have passed from the spiral which generates to the globe which is the result of the generation; and the Serpent turning on itself, taking the tail into the mouth, that symbol is the Kosmos evolved. It has formed into the globe which everywhere is the Kosmos in its manifested shape. So the Serpent becomes the Egg; then from that emerge the later forms in the Kosmos; and within that Egg sometimes instead of within the Lotus you will have Brahmâ, the creative agency. He is in the Golden Egg, which is but another symbol for the Lotus: he lives in that Egg for a while; then, coming forth from it, he creates the worlds. Hence again the symbolism of the Serpent twining round the mountain, in that churning of the ocean of substance from which, as you read in the *Purânas,* life and immortality and other things were generated; so that, as I have sometimes said, if the learned amongst you would take the *Purânas* and, studying them, would compare with them some of the statements of our Modern Science, you would be able to predict the line of scientific discovery, and in this fashion you would justify to the West, as nothing else could do, the deeper nature of the Oriental thought, showing the West the lines along which it should study and the way in which further investigations most wisely might be made.

Let me turn from that to the next point of deep interest that comes to us with regard to the Fire—an aspect of the Fire towards man—and the connection of the generating Fire in the Kosmos with that which is the root of life in the heart of the individual. Turn to the *Mundakopanishad*—I think it is the beginning of the second division—you will find the statement that "as from a blazing fire in a thousand ways similar sparks proceed, so, O beloved, are produced living souls of various kinds from the Indestructible One."[1] What is the real

[1] *Mundaka,* ii. I. 2.

meaning of that shloka? It is from Fire, which we have already seen as the central force in Kosmos, that are thrown out sparks in every direction, when the blazing Fire has reached the stage of Flame. The word "blazing" implies the stage of Flame, for it is only where the fire has begun to blaze that you have flame, and that is the note of the third of the Logoi. But the third of the Logoi is Mahat: that is, It is Intelligence in its very essence; and so we may learn that it is from Brahman *as intelligence* that these sparks are thrown out which are found within every atom of the Kosmos, so that there might be nothing in the Kosmos which is to be builded which would not have in it the essence of the Divine Life. The spark which is thrown out is the Âtmâ of the atom—which you must remember is not confined to man—the Self not of men alone, but of all beings, the innermost essence of the atom as much as the innermost essence of the highest manifested God: for the universe once more is one, and the spark which is thrown outward from the blazing fire is at the root of everything that appears in manifestation, so that the grain of sand—nay, the atoms which compose the grain of sand—has Âtmâ as its essence, and the Âkâsha as the form; which, binding as it were the ray outgoing from Âtmâ, makes manifestation by limitation and introduces the principle of division into the one. As these sparks fly outwards you have what is called in *The Secret Doctrine* a "fiery whirlwind"—a most expressive phrase—and this whirlwind passing outwards into space carries ever with it the essence of the one Fire, or the one Life. And as this whirlwind is breaking forth, there are differences in the nature of the sparks which are evolved, not in their essential nature, but in that which they bring with them into manifestation.

And here is hidden one of the greatest of the mysteries, the deepest of the mysteries, of the Occult Teaching, to which I must lead you up step by step; otherwise it will be difficult for some of you at least to follow the thought, if you have not looked beneath the letter of the Sacred Books and tried by a comparison of different passages to find out the hidden meaning that unites them all into one. Follow me step by step as I lead you to the heart of the mystery, which I do not want to state at the outset, lest by suddenly stating it, before leading you up to it, I should cause confusion of thought which might be afterwards difficult to unravel. Conceive the spark coming forth as the spark of the fiery whirlwind; conceive then that it is Âtmâ, and that the ray from this Âtmâ is cut off, as I said, by the Âkâsha, is separated, so that although fundamentally one—Âtmâ is one, and in its oneness lies the hope of our liberation—still in manifestation it becomes separated, as it were, not from its own standpoint, which is the point from which all the radiating rays are seen as one, but from the other side of manifestation, looked at not immediately as the Light, but as the Âkâsha that veils Light, and by limiting each ray makes separation, where, essentially, separation there is none. That is, looked at from within, the universe is but one; looked at from without, the universe is manifold: because it is not seen from the standpoint of Âtmâ. It is as though you stood in the central Sun, and saw along each ray, so that every part of the illuminated landscape would come to the eye through all these different rays which, standing in the centre, are seen as one light; but if you were out in the landscape, looking back along the ray, then there would be many rays around you, and you could not see the Sun through any ray save your own. Still you would see the same Sun, for all rays spread outward from the one, and in that fashion there is unity in the centre while there is impossibility of recognizing that unity so long as you are at the circumference of this mighty circle, and see as it were but along one of the rays that lead back to the centre of the whole. Now keeping that thought in mind for a moment, let us take the next step. Every atom has Âtmâ, now called Jîva, and in this sense of the term it is separate, as seen from the standpoint of the manifested individual, and no longer from the standpoint of the manifested All. This is illusion, this is Mâyâ, which we cannot transcend, and which makes the universe in a very real sense illusory; for, seeing with a vision that deceives us, seeing these separate rays in manifestation, we fail to see the unity from which they spring, and so we often find used an expression which you should no longer misunderstand, where it is said that each atom has its Âtmâ, not as implying fundamental separation, but only separation in manifestation. Having reached that standpoint, let us realize that there is now in this manifesting whirlwind of sparks a difference in nature which seems at first incomprehensible. Some of them are, as it were, living Flames—conscious and intelligent; out into this manifesting universe which is building they come as Devas. They are Intelligences which have reached a high point of spiritual development, and are far less bounded than the men who are to come into existence later. So that we find that at this early stage of manifestation there is, as it were, a whirlwind of these sparks that manifest high intelligence, so that they will be able to act as living agents of creative energy, and build the Kosmos under this coördinating and controlling force. Thus amongst the first manifestations are these manifestations of the Devas, those that are spoken of under so many names as Indra, Vâyu, and so on; those that our Orientalists say in their ignorance are "personified powers of Nature," personified in an infant civilization, personified by the child-thought of man, which, taking the external phenomena in Nature, such as air and sky and light, called them Vâyu, Indra and Agni and worshipped them as Gods!

Looked at from the true standpoint, it is not that the infant mind of man personified phenomena in Nature. It is that from the Supreme come out these sparks of Fire which are living Intelligences, which come out from Him long before an infant humanity has been born into the world at all, to build for that future humanity the Kosmos that shall be. And though it is said in the West that the folly of the untrained thinker, of infant humanity, personifies natural forces, what is really true is this: that these Devas are behind every phenomenal appearance, and are the Intelligences that guide everything that we recognize as natural laws. They are entities. They are real existences separated off from the one Âtmâ in the sense I have ascribed to the word separation, in order that they may build a universe and make that universe intelligent from centre to circumference. Phenomena in Nature—what are they? They are the outer appearances of the Devas, and the Deva is at the heart of the phenomenon; as manifestation proceeds more and more, all those in lower and lower grades are gradually evolved, until you get a hierarchy. The lowest appearance that you have on earth is only an illusory covering of the Âtmâ, so that the Soul well trained and developed, in that it is one with the creative force, can manipulate what we call Matter as it chooses, because it can control these Intelligences of which Matter is only an outer garment, and can stand as the manifested

God when once it has overcome the illusions of Matter that surround it.

And tracing onwards this great hierarchy the question arises—and here comes our difficulty—Why this difference in the manifesting sparks?—Why, as they spring forth from the blazing fire, does one appear as Deva? Why another as a lower grade of Deva? Why another as the centre round which a man is builded? Why another as the centre of a grain of sand? Why others as the centres of the atoms of which the grain of sand is builded? How in that unity that you have spoken of is there this possibility of difference in manifestation? That there is the fact of difference is the first thing to realize. Devas, men, animals, vegetables, minerals, elemental forces—these surround us and the difference is clear. The Sons of Light that we read of are the higher Devas—as I said, are the builders of the Kosmos; but we read in the sacred books of some who are called the Sons of Fire. Who are the Sons of Fire? They are the Instructors of infant humanity—those that I spoke of yesterday as teaching the infant race—as giving them their *Vedas*—as giving them all their Sacred Scriptures, as guiding them in their first efforts towards civilization, as being in a very real sense the Teachers of men. What then are they? They are Flames which have clearly brought out with them into this stage of manifestation that highly developed intelligence which enables them to become instructors of others, who are the sparks thrown out that have become incarnated in average men. It is between men in incarnation, it is between Kûmâras and men that some strange difference is suggested. Is it possible that we can discover what it means? Cycles of manifestations, comings and goings of the great Breath, Light that rebecomes Darkness, Darkness that reëmerges as Light, Souls that have become differentiated in Matter, and men that climb upwards to their source, and are liberated. They go "never to return," it is said. If they never return, why these differences in Manvantaras such as our own? Herein comes a point of the Secret Teaching which has been much lost sight of, secret because in the letter only of the published works the truth is concealed, not expressed. For what says the *Upanishad* about Brahman?

> He is concealed in the *Upanishads*, that are concealed in the *Vedas*.[1]

If you want to find Brahman, you must go beneath the words of the *Upanishads* that are written, and find the secret meaning that underlies them. There the necessity for the Guru comes in. Therefore it was said that if a man was to find Brahman, he must seek and get the great (Teachers) and attend,[2] for the mere word of the *Upanishad* itself would not reveal the God that was hidden; and it needed the Flame that had developed in

[1] *Shvetâshvataropanishad*, v. 6. [2] *Kathopanishad*, i. III. 14.

order that the spark might burn upwards and itself become a Flame. And so let us seek the secret meaning which underlies the words "never returns."

The spark in man develops (I use the word "man," meaning average humanity), that spark develops by Tapas—by burning. By what burning? By the fire of knowledge. That is the real meaning of Tapas, and in this "austerity," as it is translated constantly into English, there is the action of knowledge that burns and that purifies; and as it burns, it burns the outer sheaths of the man in which denser ignorance has its seat; and as one after another is burnt by the fire of knowledge, the Flame becomes more manifest and begins to recognize its own nature. And this spark that was smothered in Matter becomes the Flame that has liberated itself from Matter, and when liberation is complete the Flame becomes one with its source. If you take many flames and bring them together there is only one flame as they touch; for the substance is one and the division between each is lost. But let me go further with this illustration, and following out that thought, you may conceive the truth very dimly—you cannot conceive it clearly until you have been it, for you know nothing until you become it, you understand nothing until you are one with it. Human knowledge is separation, but Divine Wisdom is unity, and it is only as the outside form of the Flame disappears that it becomes merged in the One. It has not been lost. It has gained infinitely by the many Flames that have rebecome one Flame—and that is liberation. The loss of the limitation which separates you, and the widening out into all knowledge—infinite knowledge which has no limitation, is the essence of knowledge itself. But is that "for ever" in the full sense of the term? It "never returns" from Nirvâna? Those of you who have studied deeply, in the light which is thrown on this by those who know, you will have learnt that cycle after cycle is taken as limit, and that each period of non-manifestation is correlated with the manifestation that precedes it and follows it. As you have day and night taken as symbols of manifestation and non-manifestation, so you have planetary manifestation and absorption, and planetary reëmergence and absorption again, and again planetary reëmergence, until the time comes for the solar system to pass into non-manifestation. But that is correlated with the length of the solar system, and it again reëmerges, having been suspended in manifestation, and brings over to the next manifestation everything which was gathered in the preceding. And just as you learn a lesson in the day and are unconscious of that lesson in the night, but, the knowledge remaining, when you wake up in the morning you find with you the knowledge which had been acquired the day before; just as the planet passing through its period of Pralaya brings back to its next manifestation all that in the previous one it had gained; just as the solar system with its long life, passing into its long period of non-manifestation, reëmerges once more on a higher plane and becomes the solar system of a higher type, so when you deal with a Kosmos as a whole, with the Manvantara in the fullest sense of the term and the Pralaya that succeeds it, so that all Flames have become one and no longer there is differentiation, there is still a thread of Fire connecting each Flame, and when differentiation is to begin the action is on these threads of Fire that, slowly passing outwards, bring with them the Flame from out the One, and they come out with this thread of individuality which even Pralayas or Nirvânas of varying lengths cannot destroy. The One and the All have come back into manifestation, and the differences in those emerging sparks are differences which in the previous Manvantaras have been gradually developed and have been preserved even in the apparent destruction. The "never" means the length of the cycle. The "never" does not mean going absolutely out, though I have no words by which I can do anything more than make you dimly understand the sense that I am trying to convey. If it were only possible to find a word which would imply a state which is no state at all, and which I can only symbolize by taking this image of the union of the many Flames into the One, and yet the possibility of withdrawal and of each Flame bringing out individually its Karma; merged in the central Fire, but what has been called the golden thread persisting, and so preserving to the Nirvânî the possibility of future growth!

For the life of Brahman is not as the life of man. His Life, as it were, includes the infinite lives that It generates, and each of these is but as the wink of an eye to that Life which is eternal; and though as He out-breathes He breathes out the Flames, and though as He in-breathes He breathes the Flames in once more, still to Him it is but as the wink of an eyelid; and what to us is millions of years is to Him but the shortest space that we can imagine. What from that standpoint can be Nirvâna, or separation of consciousness? What from that standpoint can mean our words of Manvantara and Pralaya? It is the Infinite Fire sending out Its Flames into Space and gathering them back into Its Bosom again, and again sending them out in ceaseless undulations; hence the possibility in each successive cycle of diverging manifestations; for each brings back into the next Manvantara whatever it has gathered in the endless Manvantaras behind. And so we begin to understand that as consciousness can pass into the Turîya state and then return into limitation, so this infinite consciousness of the Kosmos may pass inward and then embody Itself once more; and that as we do not lose experience but bring it back into manifestation as we return, so what is true in miniature may be true in some transcendent sense of the Indestructible One, and His eternal life may in some sense grow richer by the innumerable experiences of innumerable Manvantaras. This ever growing evolution to us means growth: what it means to Him, none but Himself can know!

Now see how, in our own Scriptures, there are hints thrown out of that mystery; how you are told of one who is to be the Indra of the next Manvantara; how you are told of one overshadowed by Vishnu, who after the overshadowing passed away entered another stage of consciousness, and will reappear in another Manvantara as the guiding force of that. So you begin to catch the meaning when you read in the Scripture how some great devotees disappeared beneath the waters, and remained on the bed of the ocean in meditation for ten thousand years and then came back to populate the earth.[1] What are all these but efforts of Teachers to make you understand, if you will develop the intuition to listen, the inner meaning of these symbols, of these nights and days, these recurrent periods of activity and meditation; for Pralaya is the meditation of the whole, and then, out of the waters, it comes back to populate the Kosmos. So are the worlds peopled by the command of Brahmâ to some of his sons to go forth and give its population to the

[1] The ten Prachetasas, sons of Prâchînabarhis; see *Vishnu Purâna*, bk. i. chs. xiv. xv. See also *Brahma Sûtras*, Adhyâya iii. Pâda III. Sûtra 32, with Shrî Shankarâchârya's commentary thereon.

earth; for ever in Brahmâ, the Third Logos, there is the compelling Word which sends out evolved children of his. These Sons of Brahmâ, these Rishis by whom the work of creation is to be done, must come from somewhere, and you cannot have creation save where there has been slow building upwards beforehand. Those whom to-day we speak of as the Instructors of the present, in the next Manvantara will have gone onward to systems far higher than the planetary systems which we know; while the victors of the present Humanity, those who are now evolving the spark into Flame, those who by Tapas, by the fire of knowledge, are burning up ignorance and are becoming living Flames, they in the next Manvantara will come forth as the Sons of Fire—no longer as mere sparks thrown outwards, but developed Flames, who are able to build up and to instruct future races.

And now coming back from this I would venture to suggest to each of you who comes here with the desire to learn—not merely to find amusement—I would venture to suggest to any such amongst you—for there will be at least two or three such who come—that you will do well to take that thought and meditate on it for days and weeks and months, until to you it becomes a reality, for there is no other way of getting at the heart of things. You can only get the outer word from me, though I have striven in what I have been saying, to speak from mind to mind as well as from tongue to ear; you will only catch the full force of instruction and thought if you will take it into your own heart and there meditate upon it, evolving what is still concealed within.

Let us pass from that to the simpler question, which I want to give now to the outer world and not to the inner—that which is argument rather than food for meditation, still which will be useful to you in the outer world into which we shall have to go, and to which we should try to carry some light from the inner thought. I said at the very outset that Science recognizing the identity of light and sound, you might find it useful in the outside vindication of the Scriptures to point to many experiments which have been made in the scientific world, by which sound has been produced from light and light has been produced from sound. For instance, it has been discovered by some of our careful experimenters that if you will take a mass of coloured substance, and throw upon it different rays of light, some one ray will call sound from this coloured mass; that you can literally in the physical universe generate sound from colour, which is light; putting the physical colour into a ball of glass and then throwing upon it physical light, you will find that a low sound will be heard, and so you will transmute a light-ray into a ray of sound. This is an instructive experiment in the lower world which is worth keeping in mind. If you go to one who talks to you jeeringly of the Scriptures in his ignorance, you may show him that in Western Science they are coming back to this notion of identity. Again, when you see in one of your own books that when you want to communicate with the lower Devas you must speak in colour and not in verbal language, what does it mean? It means, if you have learnt the correlations of sound and colour, that what you say to the human brain by means of spoken words which throw the coarser air into motion, you speak to the more ethereal Deva in colour, which throws the astral matter of which his body is composed into vibration. So that what would be word on the physical plane is colour and light on the astral plane. If you want to communicate with a Deva who has no Sthûla Sharîra, no visible body which answers to the heavier vibrations of the air, you must understand how each sound has its colour, and when you want to communicate, you must generate colour instead of sound, for the language of the lower Gods is the language of colours, and colours to them convey what we call an articulate idea—idea on the mental plane. What speech is in the physical world, colour is in the astral world. When you read that Devas have to be spoken to in the language of colours, they will tell you "that is childish nonsense, foolish superstition; there are no Devas, no language of colours; you are all very foolish and you are talking as in the childhood of the race; it is fetishism, and you use all these words to cover your ignorance of reality." If they knew a little more—they are beginning to learn—they would find that this language of colours is a reality, and the first step has been taken in this experiment in Paris, when throwing light on coloured objects, they obtained sound.

In clairvoyance, or clear vision, when a note is sounded, a colour is seen; that is in the experience of everyone who has developed the astral sense of sight. Many people are developing it in the West to-day. There is a strange thing I have not heard of in India, that is found in Egypt. It is possible that it may not be familiar to you that some of the ancient books in Egypt were written in colours, not in the forms of letters as we have in the Sanskrit, which is the very language of the Gods. Many Egyptian books, which were meant for study by Occult Disciples, were not written in characters as we should say, but were written in colours; the understanding of them among the ancient Egyptians came to them from their great Priest-Initiates, who really were great Adepts like the Adepts of India. It is a significant thing that whenever a Sacred Book was ordered to be transcribed, if the colours were in any way altered, the transcriber was punished with death. In later times they only knew that this use of colour was a custom which had come down to them from the great Priests. They kept up the custom when the meaning that underlay the custom had passed away. The real meaning was, that whereas the outsider read the written forms, the Adept read the colours; that which conveyed one meaning by the letters, conveyed to the Occult Disciple another meaning by the colour which each letter had; so that they might publish a book which would to those who were uninitiated convey knowledge which was simply written or spoken, but the Adept taking it and reading it, had given to him that which was knowledge confined to the Occultists, for he read colours and not shapes, and each successive letter in its own colour had to him an Occult meaning. Thus the secrets of antiquity were preserved for each Initiate, who was able, when he passed his Initiation, to take over this ancient knowledge and have it as his own; and that still exists, although of course still hidden. And the language of colours is one of the stages of the training; when the student, the disciple, reads in colours and gains his teaching by different colour sensations, he learns to utilize them for the control of those forces that are known as Devas in our literature. So again you will find it written of the seven-tongued Fire—the seven tongues of Flame—which man has to understand. Turn to the *Prashnopanishad*, in which you will find the description of the life dividing itself into the vital airs. There it is said of one of these that it has seven Flames.[1] If, then, you turn to the

[1] *Prasna*, iii. 3·5.

Mundakopanishad, you will have "seven flickering tongues of the fire," each of which has its own name, and if you read those names you will find several of their names are colours.[1] That gives you the key to the understanding if you will take the passage and meditate on it, instead of trying to reach it by intellectual argumentation; for the key to that passage is in the colour of the flames, and the fact that the life distributes them over the body is a symbol to convey to your thought this hidden meaning: that life, Prâna, is the active force of that Âtmâ which has seven powers and becomes a sevenfold force in man. Each tongue of Fire becomes one of the "principles" in man, and when these are reünited in the heart, then the one flame of Âtmâ has been reached.

And so I might take you through much of symbolism, through the symbolism of the household and other fires that ought to be familiar to every thoughtful man amongst you. For why are the twice-born to study the *Vedas?* Certainly not only that they may be able to repeat shloka after shloka; the daily study of the *Veda*, which is the duty of every twice-born, surely ought to mean that in the study knowledge shall come; when he reads of the five fires that the household fires symbolize in his house, that he should know something of what they mean and be reminded of some of the hidden facts —for why is the one fire kept lighted always, and

1 *Mundaka*, i. II. 4.

from that one others are to be lighted? Why may it only be lighted by the bride and the bridegroom, and never be extinguished so long as they both remain in this earthly life? It is the ancient ideal of Hindû marriage. It is recognition of the fact in the spiritual world that when the two rebecome one, when the dual aspects of nature typified in man and woman are to be reünited, they are to form one Spirit, and it is only as they unite that they become Fire; so the outer fire lighted by the two is the symbol of the union of the Spirit that makes them one, not in order that they may find sensual gratification, but in order that they may become that Prajâpati, the creator of the future world. That is the Hindû ideal of marriage—the noblest ideal of marriage that the world has ever known. No matter how much it may have become degraded, how much it may have fallen, that it is which underlies the idea of marriage in youth before the passions are awake, that the body may not have a share in this union of the Souls and Spirits. That was the great truth on which the custom was builded, and the custom has survived where the knowledge has disappeared. For all men's Spirits coming into reïncarnation come for spiritual growth, and not for mere sensual gratification; and the Spirits that were to be joined together were not to come together by the impulses of passion in youth, that speak through the senses and not through the Spirit, and draw bodies together, no matter how little affinity there may be between the Souls that are within them. Therefore the horoscope was studied, which threw light on the nature of the life that lay before the incarnating Spirit. Therefore that was made the foundation of marriage union, and therefore there is a symbolic act in your marriage to-day, that when the bride and bridegroom are to see each other, there is a screen dropped between them so that only the eyes of one may meet the eyes of the other; for in the eye is the dwelling-place of the Spirit, and it is that which should speak from the one to the other, and no other magnetism should then pass between them. This is the ideal that underlay the ancient institution of marriage, and therefore they lighted together the fire which was the symbol of spiritual union; and therefore it is again that that fire must never be extinguished while the Spirits remained joined outwardly and within. And therefore if the wife died first, the husband gave to her the fire that she might carry it onwards into the world on the other side of death, that she might come back to him with the fire in her hands, that is, as Spirit, and he might recognize it on the other side of death and know it was his own, and that there also the two Souls were one. Now that is the symbolism that underlay the holiest of all ideals of marriage, the marriage at which the West of to-day is scoffing, and which some of the younger amongst you, blinded by your ignorance, would degrade to the lower ideal of the West, instead of purifying it again into the ancient ideal, thus giving back to India what India once had—men and women whom you cannot parallel to-day, women like those who stand in our ancient literature, noblest and purest and most glorious types of womanhood—types that you cannot find in the records of any other people, even in those pictures of imagination that are drawn by the inspiration of the poet and by the dream of the enthusiast.

Thus you might get the meaning out of the fires so familiar to you all; thus you might learn of the fires that teach you the method of reïncarnation; thus you might learn how every symbol means something to the Soul that can see. And so, Brothers, I leave with you for your own thought that which in this discourse has been so imperfectly expressed; and I leave it with the prayer for you and for myself that those Supreme Ones Who are the Fires of the Kosmos, from Whom we have sprung and to Whom we return, that we—that are but sparks that would become Flames—may by aspiration go upwards towards Them, and that as the Flame in our own heart kindles it may kindle again the fire in other Souls. Then in our land of India, the great Gods looking downward shall once more see the Fires ascending towards heaven, not the household fires which remain as symbol, but that Fire of the Spirit which, aspiring upwards towards Their Feet, shall draw us upwards towards

Them, and make India again what she should be—the very Light of the World, and the Child of the Gods. Aye! her ancient people shall be the Children of the Gods once more, and when love shall be burning in each heart as Fire, the whole will flame upward to Their throne.

Yoga.

YOGA.

BROTHERS,—In all ages, under every civilization, found within the limits of each religion, there has been an upward yearning of the Spirit of man—an attempt to find union with the Divine. It matters not what the special form of religion to which the devotee may belong; it matters not under what particular name he may worship Deity; it matters not, so far as the inner struggle is concerned, in what way he may try to express or to carry out these longings. The significant fact is that the yearning is there, a constant witness to the world of the reality of the Spirit, a constant witness of the truth of the spiritual life; the only witness, if you speak with accuracy, of the existence of the Divine, either in the universe or in man. For just as water will find its way through every obstruction, in order to rise to the level of its source, so does the Spirit in man strive upwards ever towards the source whence it came. Had it not come from the Divine, it would not seek to rise to the Divine. Were it not that it is the offspring of Deity, it would not strive to reünite itself with Deity; and the very fact that the yearning exists, the very fact that efforts, however ignorant, are made to realize it, is the constant and the perpetual witness of the Divine origin of man, is the perpetual proof of that which we were studying yesterday, that the Spark may re-become the Flame; being Flame in its origin, it may expand again into Flame, no matter how cramped it has been within the limits of manifestation.

Now the word *Yoga*, as everyone knows, means "union." It expresses in a single term everything which the Spirit can desire; for in this word "union" is implied everything; as everything comes from the Divine, so union with the Divine means possession of everything—all knowledge, all strength, all purity, all love; and the one word which implies that union marks the highest aspiration which is possible for man. I have said this aspiration is found in every religion. Take one of the most modern of religions, that which is prevalent in the West under the name of Christianity, and you will find there exactly the same attempt towards union that you find carried out so methodically in the most ancient of all religions, the Hindû. The great difference between the two is in the method. You have the aspiration in Christianity; you have not, as a rule, the training; although it is true that within the limits of a single body in the Roman Catholic Church there is some distinct knowledge as to the methods whereby union may be sought. But taking Christianity as a whole, you have aspiration, rather than sustained and deliberate effort. Yet still in reading the lives of the saints, as they are called, you will find from time to time descriptions of a state being reached, which anyone amongst you who has studied the matter would recognize as identical with the state known to us as that of Samâdhi, where consciousness passes upward or rather inward, out of the normal and into the Divine. And although that be obtained as it were by the sheer force of devotion, it is still a testimony that under each religion there is the possibility of union; as indeed we might expect to find, when we remember that all Souls are essentially one, no matter how much they may be divided by differences of birthplace or by differences of religion. And this, it seems to me, is important; important because it testifies continually to the unity that underlies different faiths, and because it tends to break down the wall of separation, which is such a barrier as far as spirituality is concerned, while it is, to some extent, inevitable as long as we remain in the purely intellectual sphere.

But what I should be prepared to maintain, as a matter of argument and of experience, is the enormous advantage of the Hindû religion in that Yoga is there understood in method as well as in object. It is not only that what the Christian calls the

"Beatific Vision" is desired, but it is that the method whereby that Vision may be reached is taught, so that the man of the world may, to a great extent, learn the steps which, taken in this life, may in a future incarnation make possible for him an advance in Yoga; while those that are prepared for further advance may, by gaining special instruction, learn step by step that which will take them onwards to the Divine.

Now it is clear that in a lecture like this, which to all intents and purposes is a public lecture—it is clear that the inner side of Yoga must be left practically untouched. Yoga, in the strictest sense of the term, is never taught, save from mind to mind, from Guru to shishya; it is not a matter for the platform; it is not a matter for discussion. Discussion has no place in true Yoga. Discussion belongs to the intellect, not to the Spirit; and Yoga is a matter of the Spirit and not of the intellect. So far as the preliminary stages go, we can deal with them from the platform; but the inner heart of Yoga is only for those who, having realized that spiritual truth is attainable, have set their whole heart on the discovery, and who go to seek it, not as controversialists into the intellectual arena, not as disputants who think themselves as good as the one to whom they nominally go as teacher, but who are willing to go to the more highly advanced in spiritual matters to learn in silence and in submission, grateful for every ray of light that comes to them, and who challenge not the light, because the Spirit in them has caught a glimpse of the source whence it comes. What I am going to try to do this morning, is to show you the preliminary stages which will gradually train a man to become capable of seeking instruction in Yoga—to point out to you what you might yourselves find out from your own Shâstras as to the published steps—if I may call them so—which lead up to the gate of the Temple; but into the Temple you must go alone to meet there your Teacher; only the pathway which leads to that gate may be shown to you, and you may begin to tread it whenever you resolve to do so.

Now in order that you may understand the intellectual side of this process of union, you need to understand your own constitution. That is the first step. It is true that the constitution of man to a very great extent only consists of the instruments whereby he may find himself. None the less must he be able to use these instruments, otherwise the preliminary steps cannot be taken; for, before you can enter on the Path at all, there are certain obstacles that have to be overcome. And those obstacles lie in your nature; they lie in the constitution of your own being. And these external obstacles must be destroyed before any real progress towards Yoga can be made. An understanding then—which will be intellectual—of your own constitution is the first step you have to take. In studying the constitution of man you need to know it, first from the standpoint of theory and then from that of practice. Because man's constitution may be looked at according as he exists in relation to the different regions of the universe, or according as he can practically divide himself when he desires to investigate these regions. These divisions may be different; but you can learn how they are correlated one to the other.

The divisions are, as I say, first theoretical and then practical. Now the fullest theoretical division is that which you may know as the sevenfold division in man that you may read in any ordinary Theosophical book: you may trace it in your own Shâstras, but you will trace it with some difficulty. Because there stress was laid rather on the fivefold division, that being the division of man as he is at present developed, the two higher stages being left out of account, inasmuch as man in his average present condition cannot possibly reach them; and it was thought not desirable at that period to confuse the mind by giving a division which could not be realizable in thought. Hints are however thrown out, so that those who passed beyond the average state of man might be able to seize the knowledge for which they had become ready; and so you will find suggestions, such as that I spoke of yesterday, the "seven-tongued flame." So you will find suggestions of seven vowel sounds; so you will find that Agni is drawn in a chariot with seven horses. So you will find that the great serpent (more often spoken of as five-headed) is occasionally spoken of as seven-headed. In this way you will catch a hint from time to time of something beyond the five—of that fivefold constitution typified by the pentacle, by the letter M, by the Zodiacal sign of Makara, the crocodile—these will hint to you that while you have these as practical reality ever to learn, there is something beyond if you have the intuition to follow the hints thus thrown out.

Now the sevenfold constitution takes Âtmâ as the Self, which, gradually unfolding, runs outward through the successive envelopes that are only differentiations of the Âtmâ. Thus you get Buddhi, spoken of as the spiritual soul; Manas, spoken of as the rational or human soul; Kâma, spoken of as the animal soul, which includes all passions and desires; and Prâna, life-principle, circulating through the ethereal body, which is unfortunately called Linga Sharîra—I say unfortunately, because the same term has a different meaning in the Hindû Scriptures. Lastly, the body itself, the Sthula Sharîra, the physical and material outside portion of man. That gives you the sevenfold division of man, or the six with Âtmâ as the seventh, Âtmâ being really the whole, but differentiating itself in its manifestation. "It willed, I will multiply."

But come to the division which will be more

familiar to many of you, in which man is regarded as Âtmâ, taking on itself five different sheaths—an exceedingly luminous classification, because in each case you have this conception of the sheath that veils the true Self; so that the real process of Yoga will be to get rid of sheath after sheath until the Self stands alone once more as it did at the beginning. According to this, you have for the body the food-sheath, Annamaya Kosha; you have then, represented in the Theosophical category by the ethereal body and Prâna—because the ethereal body is only the vehicle of Prâna—you have the Prânamaya Kosha. Then you have the double division which recognizes the duality of Manas, as you will find it taught in Theosophical books, and includes with the lower Manas, Kâma, joining together that which after death perishes, and that which passes onward to Devaloka. So that you have the Mânomaya Kosha, which includes Kâmic elements, includes passions and desires, and which takes part in the formation of the body which lasts through the Kâmalokic existence. Next as sheath for the discriminative powers of mind, comes the Vignyânamaya Kosha, thus named from *Gnyânam*, knowledge, with the prefix *Vi*, implying discrimination and analysis, a process of cutting and breaking up all the separable portions of knowledge, so that it is essentially discriminative knowledge; thus it is occasionally used to cover over the sixty-four sciences, which are classed together under that name. This Kosha then includes what the Theosophist calls Manas, this discriminative faculty in man, without the argumentative side which belongs to Lower Manas. Then you get the last of the sheaths, the Bliss-sheath—Ânandamaya Kosha—which is Buddhi—for Buddhi is essentially bliss.

Suppose instead of this classification, which deals with man as a sixfold entity, you want to know how man is going to deal with himself when he wants to investigate the different regions of the universe, you find you cannot divide him in this sevenfold or sixfold fashion. The sheaths are not all divisible the one from another. You have to take the division which is only triple. Man can only be divided into three for all practical purposes of Yoga. There are but three Upâdhis in which these different principles or sheaths can work; there is the lowest which is spoken of as Sthûlopâdhi; that includes the physical body, but is itself essentially ethereal, because the physical body can be left out of account in this matter; it has neither part nor lot save that of an obstruction that has to be gotten rid of. The real sense-organs lie in the ethereal body, and the outer casings only appear in the physical body, which to us seems so real. Then you have the Sûkshmopâdhi, or the subtle Upâdhi that is sometimes described as Linga Sharîra, or Linga Deha. It was for this reason that I said it was unfortunate that in the Theosophical nomenclature this name is applied to a lower Upâdhi, the astral or ethereal body. This Sûkshmopâdhi is the vehicle for the Kâmic and the Mânasic principles, and it is in this Upâdhi that the consciousness can make itself practically acquainted with the whole of the psychic plane. Then there is the Kâranopadhi, which is the sheath really of Âtmâ in Buddhi-Manas, and answers to the Ânandamaya Kosha, the permanent body in which what we call the immortal Triad lives throughout the Manvantara. These are the three practical divisions for Yoga, and they are correlated to the three planes of the manifested universe; the Astral plane, of which the physical is only, so to speak, the outer manifestation, so that for practical purposes the physical and astral may be regarded as one. To that the Sthûlopâdhi belongs. Then there is the psychic plane of the universe; that includes the range of passions and desires and also of intellect. To that Sûkshmopâdhi belongs. Then there is the region above it —the spiritual plane; to that Kâranopâdhi belongs. So that these three Upâdhis are correlated to the three regions of the universe—Astral plus physical —the two as one; Psychic—higher and lower; Spiritual—the highest. And the practical division is chosen for Yoga, because the consciousness may dwell in any one of these three planes, and in any one it must have a body, so to speak—a vehicle perhaps is a better word—in which it may dwell. Yoga is not possible save by the existence of these

Upâdhis in which the consciousness may work in the three great planes of the manifested Kosmos. Yoga brings about the development of these Upâdhis and their reduction under the control of the Self, so that it may dwell in one or in the other, may experience the different planes, may unify the whole. For the process of manifestation of the universe is but for the development of this unifying consciousness; the universe exists, it is said in the Scriptures, for the sake of the Soul. All is good Karma that pleases Îshvara, all is bad Karma that is displeasing to Him. For Îshvara is but the term for the Supreme Spirit, which is one with the Spirit in man. Therefore these Upâdhis are developed, in order that in their development perfect union may be secured, and the Spirit may traverse at will every plane of the universe, and have in every plane of consciousness the knowledge which belongs separately to each. That understanding then is necessary for our work.

Now comes the question: how are these planes and these Upâdhis correlated with what are called states of consciousness or conditions of Âtmâ? You will find in your Shâstras different terms applied according as the subject is taken up from the standpoint of the Âtmâ and the conditions that it assumes, or according as it is studied from without as states of consciousness. Studying states of consciousness you have the three stages, waking, dreaming, deep sleeping; or, to use the technical terms, Jâgrat, which is the normal consciousness of normal waking life; Svapna, which is the state of consciousness in what we call dream; and Sushupti, the sleep beyond dream—the dreamless sleep we call it. There is indeed a fourth, the Turîya state, but that is not a state of consciousness in manifestation. That is the widening out of the limited consciousness into the all. And therefore it lies beyond this question of vehicles, for in that Âtmâ exists as Âtmâ. It has thrown off every sheath until it has found itself. As long as we are dealing with the Upâdhis, with sheaths, we have the three without the Turîya state; no condition remains in the Turîya state. Man may reach it, but he carries thither no vehicle. It is the state of liberation. It is the state which is entered by the Jîvanmukta; but the Jîva either passes finally onwards out of all vehicles, or passing into it as Jîva, pure and simple, returns to the vehicle on leaving it; the vehicle cannot be carried into it; for it is beyond limitation; it is the One and the All. Now turn to the *Mândûkyopanishad*, that one which is so short, but is so priceless, if you will take it and meditate upon it and so find its inner meaning. There you read not of states of consciousness but of conditions of Âtmâ. First comes Vaishvânara, correlated to the waking state, for in that Âtmâ cognizes the external world. You are told it is in contact with external bodies, that is the nature of this condition. It is then of course in the Sthûlopâdhi, the lowest of the three vehicles. It passes out of that into the state of splendour, that is the Taijasa condition. In that it studies the internal objects, you are told. The Upâdhi for this is the Sûkshmopâdhi; it dwells in the inner world. It passes once more out of that into the state of knowledge, Pragnyâ; then it is said that knowledge is uniform; then it is said that its nature is Bliss, its mouth is Knowledge.

A most significant and luminous statement, worthy of your careful consideration. Its nature Bliss; that implies the presence of the Ânanda-maya Kosha. Its mouth Knowledge; that implies, if you will think of it, the suggestion of the presence of that which may become, but is not, the spoken word; the potentiality of the speech without the speaking, for speech belongs to the lower plane. Its mouth is knowledge: the mouth is there, but the nature is bliss; when the Âtmâ comes outwards from that state, then it passes downward into the realm of speech, and the mouth may utter the spoken word, but there is no word on that plane. There is the potentiality of sound, but not the sound itself. And then there is the fourth. Of that fourth there is nothing said save negatives, for it is indescribable. It is Âtmâ in itself, Brahman in itself. It is the sacred Word as one; no longer as the separated letters. You are given the three letters, A, U, M; each of these being correlated to a condition of the Âtmâ; finally the one-sounded word is spoken; because the Âtmâ has re-become the one and no separation of letters can then exist. So, see even by that outward explanation how much there is of teaching in the printed book. And that is only the outer explanation. You have to find out for yourselves what underlies suggestion after suggestion; but taking it in that form it puts you on the way towards Yoga, for it gives you the three stages, the three steps, the three conditions of the Âtmâ.

And the practical way of realizing those? Of that also we may learn something; although not much when we are dealing with it in a fashion so imperfect as the present. Now let us seek the preparatory stages to make all this theoretical knowledge practical to some extent: at least so far as to make it possible, as I said in the beginning, for the man living in the world with household duties, social duties, and national duties, to prepare himself for the real life. This at least we may take into consideration, with a few hints of what lies beyond. Clearly it will be impossible for a man to spring from the average life of men into the practice of real Yoga. To do that would only mean inevitable failure; for although intense desire might carry a man into the beginning of it, there would never be the tenacity which would hold through the shocks which follow the first enthusiastic springing forward into the inner life. You cannot make a sudden step without an equally sudden reäction. You cannot spring high without the shock of re-descending to the earth. Therefore the wisdom of the ancient Sages did not permit a man to enter straightway into the ascetic life. It was forbidden save in the exceptional case where an advanced Soul came into reïncarnation, and from birth or earliest childhood special capacities were seen. The ordinary life was a carefully graduated life, in which a man might take up just as much of religion as he felt the inner impulse to take up. The life was a religious life, and religious ceremonies accompanied it throughout, but a man might throw as much spiritual energy as he chose into the ceremonies. He might repeat them as a matter of form, and even then they would remind him of the life beyond the physical; or he might throw into them a little devotion, and then they would lead him a step further; or he might throw his whole heart into them, and then they would be a real preparation for the later life. If that were done, if the life of the Grihastha—the householder—were over, and every duty had been accomplished, then he might pass onwards, if he would, into the life of the hermit, into the life of the ascetic; because by these graduated practices he had prepared himself for the finding of the Guru and for the leading of a truly spiritual life.

The first step that is always laid down as a preparation for Yoga is the ceasing from wicked ways. A very commonplace step; a mere truism in every religion; but the fact that it is a truism does not make it less true. And since no Yoga is possible without it, save the Yoga that leads to destruction, the first step is purification of the life and the ceasing from wicked ways. Whosoever has not ceased from wicked ways, thus beginning the Yoga which goes on to the subduing of the senses and of the mind, whosoever has not ceased from wicked ways cannot find Âtmâ. That, then, is the first and most commonplace step, and every one—if you tell them it is a necessary preliminary—almost every one shrugs his shoulders and says "of course"; but he does not practise it. Until he does, no practice in Yoga is possible. Nothing but talk is possible until a man has begun to purify his life; until he is truthful in thought as well as in speech; until he cannot be persuaded to swerve from the path of rectitude by any outside temptations; until the whole of his thought and desire at least is towards the right; until, however often he falls he recognizes a fall as a fall, and tries to rise again; until he has made at least the attempt to form a righteous ideal and to carry out that ideal practically in life. I say this is the most commonplace of all religious teachings, and the one which is the hardest at first to carry into practice. Now for the enormous majority of men who do not take up this as a rule of life, for the enormous majority Yoga is and can be nothing more than a word; any attempt to practise it is like an attempt to run before learning to walk; and the only possible result is the result which the child has when it is in too much hurry to walk—it falls down and falls down until it learns caution and gains equilibrium.

I say this because there are very many practices which may be learned without purity of life, but these will lead to mischief and not to good. It is far easier to take up a book on Yoga and put into practice for a few minutes, or for an hour or two, or for a day, some particular thing that you may read there, than it is to keep a constant watch over the daily life and purify it at every moment of the day. Far easier, but also far less useful; and the discipline of the body and the mind is the first stage in practical Yoga. In daily life all sorts of methods of discipline may be found, and when a man has really determined to discipline mind and body, he will, through his daily life as opportunities occur, make for himself some definite rules—it does not matter what the rules are, provided they are harmless—and he will rigidly keep these rules after he has made them. That is to say, he will systematize his life; he will determine certain points of time, and at those points he will force himself to do the things that he has previously decided shall be the occupation of that particular moment or hour. Let me take a very common illustration. He fixes an hour for rising, but when the hour comes somehow he fails to rise. He is lazy, or sleepy, or what not. Now it does not matter in itself whether he rises a quarter of an hour earlier or later than the hour fixed, but it does matter that he shall do what he has determined to do. For the carrying out of a resolution in the face of disinclination strengthens the will—and no progress in Yoga is possible unless the will is strong and the body and mind obedient; this power may be best accumulated in the practice of daily life. And when the mind and body are controlled, brought to obedience, no matter what may be the temptations of sloth or anything else, he has taken the first step on this path of Yoga; for they have been made obedient to something that is higher than themselves. By strengthening the will, the man is making one of the instruments that he is going to use in his further progress. Then take the question of food, not a vital question, but one of considerable importance; you will find certain kinds of foods forbidden to those who lead a spiritual life. Food should be correlated to the purpose for which you are living. There is no one rule which you can lay down for all. There are rules which are different according to the purposes that you are using your life to accomplish. According to that which it is the desire of your life to accomplish, so should be the food that you take to nourish, to keep, the life of the body. Therefore it was that when to be a Brâhman meant to be a man who had made progress in the spiritual life and who desired to advance rapidly and further along the road, the rules as to what he might and might not do were exceedingly stringent; and then it was that he was told to eat those things that have the Sattvic quality, because he did not want to bring into the body which he was endeavouring to purify any foods having the Râjasic or the Tâmasic qualities, which would draw him downward instead of lifting him upwards. It is true that the body is the lowest part of us, but it is not for that fact to be neglected. It is important to lighten your weight if you have to climb. Though the weight does not help you upwards, the lessening of the weight will make the upward climbing less difficult than otherwise it would be. And that is all that you have to do in dealing with the body. It does not help you to spiritual life; but it holds you back. And you want to lessen the hold of the body as much as possible. That is really the use of an external observance. If there is nothing but the external, if there is no upward rising, it is almost a matter of indifference whether the weight is heavy or light, for it is always going to remain on the ground, and it is the ground that bears it, and it does not hold anything down. Tie a rock to a post. It does not matter whether the rock be heavy or light, for the post has nothing in it that will rise. But tie a rock to a balloon which is striving to rise upwards, and as you lessen the weight of the rock, the possibility of rising will come to the balloon, until ultimately the power that draws it upward is greater than the dead weight of the rock that holds it down, and it will go upwards carrying the rock with it, because it has overcome its resistance. That is the way in which the body and all outward observances should be regarded. That is why when the Spirit is free all outward forms become matters of indifference. The very rites and ceremonies of religion that are binding on the Soul that is still unliberated, become useless when the Soul has gained liberation, for then the Soul no longer can be held by anything. And as the rites of religion are meant to be the wings which will lift the Soul upwards against weight, when the weight has vanished and the Soul is free, it no longer needs these wings. It is in its own atmosphere, where equilibrium has been gained, and neither upward nor downward has any meaning for it; for it is at the centre which is the All.

I say this because it is a thing that ought to guide your judgment, if you *will* judge your neighbours. It would be far better if you never judged them at all. What right of judgment has any one of you as concerns one of your brothers? What know you of his past? What know you of his Karma? What know you of the conditions that surround his life? What know you of his inner struggles, his aspirations and his faults? What right have you to judge him? Judge yourself, but do not judge another; for when you condemn any, judging him only from without and by one or another external observance that he may or may not use, you injure yourselves far more than you injure him; you are judging in the lowest sphere, and you are injuring all your own inner sphere and clouding it over by the tendency of unkindness and of lack of compassion.

Now it is in connection with this dealing with the body that a large number of external observances have been advocated and practised—many of them exceedingly useful and some of them exceedingly dangerous. Take a practice which is a very useful one, and which is not dangerous but helpful when practised in moderation in a country like this, with a very long physical heredity behind it and the practice of thousands of generations; that which is known as Prânâyâma—the checking of the breath—a practice known to almost every Brâhman at least. This is done with a very definite purpose, with the object of shutting out all external objects and withdrawing the soul from the senses to the mind—the first stage in practical Yoga. The shutting of the various senses physically, the checking of the breath physically, these are really the lightening, so to speak, of the weight, and making it easier for the mind to retire from the external world. But where these directions, which have been published to some extent, are suddenly taken up by people not fitted to practise them by physical heredity, and when they are carried out with much persistence and with Western energy, without someone who knows how to guide the student, the practice may become exceedingly dangerous. If it is carried beyond a certain point it may seriously affect the organs of the body and may cause disease and death. Therefore, even for you who are Asiatics it is never wise to pursue this practice very far unless you are under the training of some one who understands it thoroughly, and who is able to check you the moment you touch danger. Whereas for the European it is unwise to practise it at all, because he has not any suitable physical heredity, nor are the physical and psychical surroundings amongst which he lives fitted for a practice which may be said to work on the physico-psychical life; thus the practice may be exceedingly dangerous, and for a European who is going to begin, the physical training will begin in a different fashion. There again is a point where judgment would be exceedingly unjust; because unless you take these circumstances into consideration, you may be blaming the man for what? Because he does not do a thing which in him would produce dangerous bleeding of the lungs; and so would entirely take away from him the physical garment in which, if more carefully trained, possibly progress might be obtained.

Of course this may be carried very much further in what is called Hatha Yoga. You may see it carried to the furthest extreme in those cases of the ascetics where some particular practice is adopted —whether that of raising the arm and holding it up till it withers; or clenching the hand till the nails grow into the flesh; or gazing at the sun; or doubling the body, and so on—an enormous number of different practices that some of you must have yourselves seen from time to time. Is there or is there not any value in these practices? How is it that we see them adopted? What is their object and what their real worth? Now it would not be true to say that they are without value. First of all they have this value, that in an age like our own they are constant and standing witnesses to the strength of the inner aspiration which overcomes all bodily passion and all physical temptation in order to seek after something which is recognized as greater than the physical life. It is not fair to omit from sight in judging these cases that service which they do to humanity. For in the world, where almost everyone is seeking after things of the world, where ambition is for money, for place, for power, for fame, for the praise of men, it is not without value that a few should even act in this fashion, and throwing everything that men love aside, proclaim by the very fact of their tortured existence the reality of the Soul in man, and the worth of something which is above the anguish of the body. So that I do not think that anyone should speak lightly of the folly of these men, even though he disagree with them, even though he disapprove of them, even if he say that their method is not right. In any case you should recognize the strength of the devotion which can trample on the body in seeking after the Soul. Even if the method be mistaken, as I myself believe it to be mistaken, still it is a nobler life even in its blunders than the commonplace seeking after transient objects; for it is nobler to seek the higher and climb after it and fall, than it is to seek things only of the earth, to waste everything in gaining those transient objects.

And there is the side, another side, which will bring to them their reward in a future incarnation. It is true they will by these methods never reach the spiritual plane. It is true that by these methods they will never reach the higher spheres of existence. Yet it is also true that they are by these methods developing the strength of will that in their next birth may carry them far along the road. Has it ever struck you what their strength of will must be; not in the stages when the posture has become automatic, but in the early stages, when every moment is a moment of torture? That is the time when the Soul is developed, and when if you pay the price of pain you may purchase that which you pay for. They pay it for strength of will, and that strength of will must come back to them in their future life. And it may be that the strength of will shall then be enlightened by the devotion which made them follow such a life, and that the two together may open up the path towards real knowledge. Although for this incarnation they may fail in reaching the spirit, yet in another devotion and will combined may carry them far, far beyond those who think themselves wiser, because they are not fanatical—as I frankly think these men are. You may say to me, "Are we to follow the practice?" No; for I have already said I regard it as a mistake. I only mentioned this view because I hear so much of idle scoff, so much of idle jeer, from men who are not fit to come within a mile of those who have at least recognized and tried to follow the possibility of spiritual life.

And then there is one word to be said of another life, a life which is not of absolute self-torture, but which is that of complete withdrawal from the world to the forest. That has been said to be a selfish life; in very many cases it is connected with selfishness, but not always. Those lives that are spiritual keep up the spiritual atmosphere which prevents the country as a whole from falling as low as it otherwise would. They keep up the recognition of the reality of a spiritual life which may be stimulated into activity, and the fact that India has a possibility of revival in herself is largely due to those recluses of the forests and of the jungles, who have kept possible a spiritual atmosphere into which vibrations may be thrown which then may strike on the outer lives of men.

For what is the underlying truth of Hatha Yoga? It is this; that when growth is complete, body will be the obedient servant of the Spirit, and will be developed along the particular lines which will give to Spirit the organs in the body whereby it may work on the outside universe of Matter. That is the real truth of all Hatha Yoga practices. They train the body. They throw into activity certain centres—certain chakrams as they are called—they throw them into activity, and these centres are to act as the organs for the interior life. They are the organs whereby the inner life may work on the material universe, and whereby what are called phenomena may be brought about. Phenomena cannot be brought about by the Spirit at its highest working directly on what we call Matter at its lowest, that is by Âtmâ working directly on the material universe; the gulf is too great, it has to be spanned. And if you are to control the physical universe and physical laws, it is necessary to develop certain material organs and astral organs in connection with the body which, brought into immediate contact below with the physical universe, and in contact above with the mind and Spirit, will enable the Spirit working downward, so to say, to bring about the physical results that it desires. Now Hatha Yoga is the recognition of this truth and the bringing it into practice on the lower plane. It works first on the body and develops a great many of those organs into control over these inner forces. It makes the body easy to be thrown into a condition which does respond to subtler vibrations, and it subjugates the body.

So one who practises Haṭha Yoga can, with comparative ease, obtain control over certain forces of the material universe. It wakes up the astral body, it throws the astral centres into vibration; so that there again, powers are gained of a most extraordinary character, so far as the outer world is concerned. But the powers are bad in this sense—that by beginning from below and stimulating these organs, the physical and astral bodies, without the corresponding action in the mind and the Spirit, the limit of action is soon reached. It is artificial stimulation instead of a natural and evolutionary one. Those organs should be stimulated from above and not from below, if they are to persist life after life; and by the Hatha Yoga practices they are stimulated into action from below, just as in hypnotism you begin by paralyzing the outer senses; thus you gradually lead to atrophy and to permanent paralysis. Hatha Yoga practices, long continued, make Râja Yoga impossible for that incarnation. That is why objection is raised to them in many of the wisest of our books. That is why it is said that Râja Yoga is the thing to be sought after and why Hatha Yoga is discountenanced. It is not that no physical practices are ever needed. It is not that these psychic powers are not ultimately to be evolved; but it is that they are to be evolved as the natural result of the developing Spirit, and not as the artificially stimulated results of the body first and then of the astral form. To begin at that end means limitation to the psychic plane. To begin on the spiritual means the unifying of all planes into one. That is the essential difference between the two forms of Yoga. Râja Yoga is more difficult and it is the slower, but it is certain. Its powers are carried over from birth to birth, whereas beyond the psychic plane it is not possible to progress by using the purely Hatha Yoga methods.

And now I want to put to you one or two general statements as regards these practices, as I will now call them, that may wisely be used in daily life. You may remember in the *Aitareyopanishad* that after man is formed he is *vitalized*—if I may use a somewhat commonplace expression—by the Devas, and that then the Supreme Soul asks the question: "How shall I enter in?" and he enters in at the place where the hairs of the head divide, that is, the Brahmarandra, the centre of the skull. He takes up three places; in the right eye, in the "inner organ," and in the heart: three places in which he abides. These places are significant. The right eye stands for the senses; the inner organ for the brain and its mind; the heart for the inner self. And he enters into these one by one, first into the eye, that is, to the senses; then into the inner organ, that is, to the mind; then into the heart, that is, to the final dwelling place in which he resides. That is the keynote to all these triple divisions that I gave you at the beginning. Each of these belongs to one or other of these stages and conditions of which I spoke; and when we begin to practise, it is these that we take up as the stages that may be practised in the world before the Guru is found; which any one of you may begin to practise, and so make possible for yourselves the later stages when you have succeeded in mastering these. First then in seeking the Soul you will deal with the senses. You may choose some image in the mind, and concentrate upon that, until no stimulus can reach you from without. This is the concentration of the mind within itself and withdrawal from the senses. Why should not a man practise that daily? Why should he not get into the habit of being able to withdraw the mind from working in the senses; so that it may be thrown back into itself and work only within the limits of the mind? All great men of thought do it as a matter of natural instinct. All great thinkers do it. Take the thinkers who have given to the world great literary works and read their lives, and you will find that it was a constant fact that when they were occupied with great mental problems they became oblivious of the body; that they would sit thinking, missing their meals, sitting through the whole day, sometimes the whole of the night; oblivious of every want of the body, even the want of sleep, because they had withdrawn the mind from the senses and had concentrated it within itself.

This is the condition of all fruitful thought, it is the condition of all fruitful meditation. Meditation is more than this indeed. But this is its first beginning, for you want to draw the Soul away from the senses; otherwise it keeps going outward and you want it to come inwards towards its own seat. Therefore stop the senses. Without that no further progress is possible. And then from the worldly standpoint it will be useful even; for this concentration of mind that you find advocated in old books as a preliminary stage of Yoga, is a condition of the most effective mental work. The man who can concentrate is the man who can conquer the intellectual world; he who can bring all his faculties to a single point becomes one-pointed, as Patanjali has it. That is the one who is really capable of making progress intellectually. You cannot push a wide object through obstacles; you must bring it to a point and it will easily pierce through all. So it is with the mind. If the mind is scattered through the senses it is diffused. There is no propelling force that can send it through obstacles. Bring it to a point, and then the force behind it will push it through. Thus even in common intellectual matters concentration is the condition of success. But this carried out thoroughly brings you to the second stage, the Svapna stage, then the condition is that of the mind being fixed on the internal objects; that is, you fix the attention on concepts and ideas and not on the objects which gave rise to them. No longer on the outer body but on that which you have drawn from it into the mind; and you study the internal objects, which are the concepts, the ideas, the deductions and abstract thoughts which from the outer world you have collected. The more perfectly you can do it, the nearer you are coming to the completed Svapna stage, and when you can do it well you have really made one stage onward in the Yogic method, for you have gained the power of bringing the soul into the internal organ, and once there further progress may be gained. The next stage, still within the limit of Svapna, is not only to withdraw the mind into itself, but to hold it there against the intrusion of thoughts which you do not desire. Suppose you have already secured it against the intrusion of outside stimuli, and the senses can no longer bring you out of this state of concentration; but perhaps thought can do it. The mind itself may not be thoroughly guarded against such intrusion. It is withdrawn from all possibility of stimulation from without. It may be so strong that a man coming up and touching you would not bring you out of the state of perfect abstraction; but still within itself it may not be equally steady, and an idea may reach it while a sensation cannot. On its own plane a thought may intrude. That is the next stage of concentration. You must be able to kill thoughts. The moment a thought comes, if it is not wanted it must fall away. First you kill it by deliberate action; that is, you reject it when it comes. But the realizing of its presence is lack of concentration. The very fact that you see it there shows that it is able to make an impression upon you. Therefore you must deliberately kill it. Therefore when the thought comes to you you must throw it back. This will be a long process; but if you keep doing it month after month, nay, year after year, at last it will become automatic, and you will have made in the mind such a repellent power that you may set that power going by drawing yourself into the centre, and the thought coming from the outside and striking against it will get self-thrown back. It is like a wheel revolving very rapidly. If it is slowly moving, any moving body that may come against it may check its revolution. If it is moving very rapidly, any moving body that comes against it will get itself flung off. And in proportion to the rapidity of the revolution will be the force of repulsion with which that body is thrown back. That becomes automatic, and just as you get beyond the stimulus of the senses, you get beyond the reach of the mind: that is, the mind becomes self-centred and the circumference throws off automatically everything which desires to enter. That is the position which you have now secured. There again there is the worldly advantage, for the highly concentrated mind does not wear itself out; it does not allow to enter all the thoughts which it does not require. It does not consider them. It does not allow energy to be wasted on them, and so fritter away its powers. It is kept empty as to thought when work is not required, instead of being a sort of ever busy machine, always going, and so wearing itself out. Instead of this, it is a machine under absolute control, which works or does not work exactly as the Self desires that it shall or shall not.

Beyond this stage no conscious progress is possible without the help of a Teacher. Conscious progress, I say, but unconscious there may be, for the Teacher may be there though you know him not. But there is one way still in which progress may be made, although unrealized in a sense, without your knowing that any one is helping you, but that is not by knowledge. If you still desire to tread the path of knowledge you must find your Teacher. But there is something in the world which is stronger than knowledge, and that is devotion. For that is the Spirit itself; and while I have been dealing with all that which consciously you can do, there is one other thing that you can also do which will help you. And that is to open wide all the gates of the Soul, so that you no longer shut out the sun, so that the sun of Spirit may stream in and purify and enlighten, without any action of your lower self. Now devotion is the opening of the windows of the Soul. It does nothing. It is an attitude. Devotion means that you realize something which is greater than yourselves, something which is higher than yourselves, something which is sublimer than yourselves, towards which your attitude is no longer an attitude of criticism, no longer an attitude of what you call learning, no longer any attitude save that of prostration, throwing yourself down before it in worship, and remaining silent to hear if any word may come. By that, progress is possible into the innermost recesses of the Spirit, for devotion opens the way for the light to come in; the light is always there, we do not make it. These processes that I have been speaking about are the tearing off of sheath after sheath, so that we may consciously recognize the light. It may seem to get brighter as sheath after sheath is torn off. It does not really get brighter; it is there; but *we* fail in the outer recognition of the light within. Devotion breaks through all sheaths from within; and then the light streams forth; and it has nothing to do but shine. It is the quality of light to shine. It is we who obstruct it, and make its shining out impossible. And therefore it is that in the ignorant man you will sometimes find a spiritual knowledge that transcends the intellectual knowledge that some great genius may have obtained. He sees the heart of things. Why? Because the inner light is streaming forward and the devotion has opened the eye into which light comes, and it sees along the beam right into the recesses of the sanctuary. Not by knowledge only may be opened sheath after sheath; love too is needed, that the man may find himself, and breaking through them all, one by one, may at last open out the way to the Feet of the God. And that is possible everywhere, not only in forest and jungle, if man can separate himself from the things of earth. For this no outer renunciation is necessary; it is the deeper renunciation by the Soul of all the objects of sense and of the world. It is that which Shrî Krishna means when he speaks of devotion. Meditation means this opening out of the Soul to the Divine and letting the Divine shine in without obstruction from the personal self. Therefore it means renunciation. It means throwing away everything that one has, and waiting empty for the light to come in. It means non-attachment to the fruit of action. Everything you do, you do because you are in the world, and your duty is to perform actions. Shrî Krishna said, "I am ever acting!" Why? Because if He did not the revolving wheel would stop. So with the devotee; he should do his outer actions, because they are examples to other men; because his Karma has placed him in the world where these duties claim discharge. But it is not *he* who does them. Once devotion is attained, the senses move towards their appropriate objects; mind also moves towards its appropriate objects; but the devotee—he is neither the senses nor the mind. He is the Self that is recognized as Lord. And so he is always worshipping, while the senses and the mind are busy with the external and the internal objects. That is the meaning of non-attachment. He is not attached to any of the works which his senses bring about; let them go and do their work, and do it with the utmost perfection. Let his mind also go into the outer world and do its share in the world's work. It is not himself; he is ever worshipping at the Feet of his Lord. While he is there, external things may do their work; what power of attachment have they to bind him to any of their actions? But to reach that state non-attachment must be deliberately practised; you must learn to be indifferent to results, provided you do your duty, leaving the outcome in the hands of the mighty forces that work in the universe, and that only ask of you to give them the outer material in which they may clothe themselves while you remain one with them. To do this you must be pure; to do this you must always have the heart fixed on the one reality. The devotee is ever within, in the heart. He is always within the shrine, and the mind and body are busy in the outer world. That is true Yoga; that is the real secret of Yoga.

For all that it is perfectly true that there is a stage in which knowledge once more comes in, and the devotee may learn from his Guru how to become a conscious co-worker with the spiritual forces. He may be a worker before he is conscious of it, only by means of devotion. Conscious co-working implies knowledge. It means that the Guru takes the shishya in hand and teaches him how he may more perfectly purify himself and remain utterly unsoiled by the touch of actions in which he works. While conscious co-working is joy unutterable, co-working at all makes life worth living.

I should not deem it worth while to keep you this morning studying a subject such as this, were it not that it seems to me that one of you here or there may possibly catch some thought of devotion which shall make the way into the inner sanctuary easier and clearer for you than it was before. I have been dealing intellectually with these sheaths of the Soul, intellectually with these regions of the universe, intellectually with these states of consciousness, intellectually with the methods by which progress may be made. I should do less than my duty here to you if I left you on the intellectual plane. Therefore I venture these words as to the essence of Yoga, no matter what the outer form may be; I venture to say to you—to some of you it will seem folly and fanaticism, but what matters that to me?—I venture to say to you that devotion is the one thing that gives security; devotion is the one thing that gives strength; devotion is the one way that opens up the road to the innermost where the Divine is manifest. Better worship ignorantly in devotion than refuse to worship at all.

Better bring a flower or leaf to some village God, as the poorest of those that come ignorantly and desire to give out of their poverty, than be some great intellectual genius that the world honours, too proud to bow before that which is higher than itself, too intellectually strong to bend its knee before the spiritual life; for Spirit is higher than intellect, as intellect is higher than the senses. Spiritual life is the highest life, and it is open to everyone, for the Spirit is the innermost core in each, and none may deny its presence in any man. Cultivate then reverence, reverence for everything which is noble; cultivate worship, worship of that which is divine; and then when the body and the senses fail you, then when the mind breaks down and has nothing more to give you, then that eternal Spirit, which is the life of your life, the Soul of your Soul, then That shall rise stronger, because the body and the mind have perished, and going upward it shall find itself—nay, it need not go; it is there already, always—it shall find itself lying at the Lotus Feet of its God: there where there is no illusion, no separateness, no pain: there where all is bliss. For the very essence of the Divine is love and is joy, and that is the heritage of the Spirit, greater than anything that the passing world may give.

SYMBOLISM.

Symbolism.

Symbolism in religions may be called a common language. By this it is meant that certain external forms are taken, which, presented to the view of anyone versed in the forms, convey to the mind of that person a definite idea; just as, for instance, you may have an ideographic language which is read by each person into his own tongue; just as you may have numbers in arithmetic, each number carrying some idea, but if the number be put into spoken word, the word will differ according to the language which is employed. So, in all ages have men who have studied religions had a common language by which they could communicate with each other; so that no matter what might be the country of the person, no matter what might be the particular religion that exoterically surrounded him, when he came across the symbol, he recognized its meaning, and so had knowledge conveyed to him by his fellow Initiates, which to him was as definite and as certain as though it had been conveyed in his own particular language of words.

Now of the underlying unity of religions there can be no greater proof than the identity of religious symbols. When you find within a Hindû temple the same symbols as you find in far-off ruins in Western lands; when you find the same symbol that is in the temple and in the Western ruins reproduced in the modern Christian cathedral or church; when you find in Asia, in America, in Europe and in many of the islands of the Pacific Ocean, just the same symbol reäppearing; then you may know that the people who made the symbol held the same notion, used the same means to convey it, knew the same truth, and worshipped the same idea. And in this fashion, the study of symbolism may constantly enable us to gain from the past knowledge that has slipped away in the present. Thus we may know some great truth which conveys sustenance to our own thinking, and taking up some ancient Scripture, we may recognize under the garb of symbol, the truth which in some other fashion we have received. So taking the ancient books, which were written by great Sages, by Divine Instructors, we may find that they have hidden in these books secrets of spiritual knowledge, and that they have done it in order that the secrets might be preserved amongst all the changes and chances of life; and that when a man has reached a certain stage of spiritual evolution, there might be here ready to his hand knowledge that he might acquire. Thus what has been carried through ages of darkness may once again appear for the enlightening of the world. Inasmuch as to-day we are in a cycle of darkness, as we are living in that Kali Yuga, during which spirituality is at its lowest ebb, and inasmuch as this period is characterized by the triumphs of the powers of darkness and the blinding of the insight of man which in happier ages is clear and distinct, symbolism is to us of deepest moment. For when this cycle was approaching, it became necessary that the Sages should hide under symbol and under garb of outer fables those truths which were to be preserved for generations to come—not only in what we call ordinary symbolism or outer form, but also in allegory, in fable, in that which is regarded as myth, and in that which is used as ceremony. In all these things there is the heart of spiritual truth, and from time to time, some one arises who is able to see the truth underneath the outer symbol of fable or ceremony; and so bringing out the truth from the symbol, is able to strengthen man's belief in spiritual realities, and reässert in the midst of darkness the light of a happier time. For not only does symbol carry on truth from age to age, but it also acts as a constant witness for the existence of the truth. Sometimes it may be meant to hide it, but at other times it is meant that the hidden truth shall be brought out, so that the bringing out may reëstablish man's belief in truth. The special work that is being done to-day by the

Theosophical Society is done at the will of those Divine Instructors who devised the symbols and gave them in charge to the various religions of the world. So that from time to time what is to be done, and is being done to-day, is that when truth has been lost to the majority and when belief in it has largely disappeared, some one taking hold of the symbol shall explain it; then the reasonableness of the explanation recommends itself to the minds of men, and they feel the evidence of the existence of truth, because it is brought out, as it were, from its hidden recesses; then faith grows up again, and belief is once more able to lift up its head, because the unveiling justifies the reality of the symbol and they recognize the inner truth, and so become convinced of the light which was hidden, and which by the opening, as it were, of the lantern is once more revealed to the world. So that symbolism has this value of not only carrying on the truth, and of giving it to those who are wise, but also of impressing on the outer world the persistent reality of the spiritual truth; and it is the knowledge of this which makes some of us lay stress on the preservation of ceremonies, even when they are not understood. I know that in the minds of some, this seems folly and superstition; I know that in the minds of some, this seems to be raising an obstacle in the way of progress. They only see the ceremony from the standpoint of the obstacle; they do not realize the value that within that seeming obstacle may be enshrined. Sometimes there may be an ancient monument which tells of the past history of the people. You want to carry a railway through it, and you will say that it is very important that the railway should be a straight line between two points, and that it is far better to sweep away the ancient monument which has become an obstruction, and to allow the people to have the practical advantage of saving ten minutes of time, which will be lost if the railway goes round the monument. Instead of pulling it down and destroying it, it may sometimes be wiser to waste ten minutes' time—when so much time is wasted—than to destroy the records of an event that otherwise might pass without record out of the minds of men. So if the ceremonies, whose meaning even has been lost—lost for the present from the eyes of ordinary men, but not lost from the knowledge of spiritual Sages, and not lost in their future power, when once more the truth that they hide is revealed—if the ceremonies of Hindûism had been entirely swept out of India, where should we find the arguments for the reäffirmation of spiritual truth to the Indian people? But inasmuch as the ceremonies have remained and inasmuch as the symbols still exist, then, coming with knowledge, we can justify the ancient teaching even by these preserved symbols, and so can reach the hearts and minds of the people in a way that would be utterly impossible if the symbols had disappeared.

Now as an illustration, let me begin with one symbol which is universal and found in every religion, although in different religions differing very slightly in the shape in which it appears—I mean the famous symbol of the Cross, largely identified to-day in the modern world with a very modern religion, largely identified probably in the minds of many of you with that religion. It is none the less the most ancient of all the symbols, and has come down to us from a time lost to Western thought in obscurity. No matter how deeply you dig into the crust of the earth; no matter how ancient the ruins of the city that, by such digging, you may unbury; no matter whether you dig into that crust in America, in Europe, in Asia, and in Africa; everywhere you will find the Cross. There are places in Europe that have been unburied by modern investigation, places that are covered over with the ruins of civilizations which had absolutely disappeared from the surface of the earth long before the civilization of the Roman Empire was dreamed of—a civilization that endured for centuries and then fell into ruin.

Passing back over the millenniums and digging down through those ruins that tell of its decay, down through them all into still older ruins of a civilization that has left no trace, save in these deep buried records; even there you shall find a Cross marked on pottery that has long outlasted the very bones of the people that made it; for the pottery, found beside little heaps of dust that vanish when the tomb is opened, has graven on it the symbol of the Cross, and buried by the side of the dead conveys its own sacred signification. Go back as far as you will into the antiquities of this—the most ancient of all lands so far as the Fifth Race of man is concerned—there is no place where you will not find this symbol; in the most ancient of the Scriptures you will find the Cross, representing, in later times, the circle of the horizon, representing farther back the form of Vishnu, which is Time. The circle symbolizes Time unending, and within it a Cross on which lie all Gods, all Rishis, all Suns and all Stars, everything which is in the manifested universe. Go farther back, before the Fifth Race is born—back into those times of which no record remains, save in the hands of the Initiates themselves—here and there is a rock of which they only can explain the meaning, and on these rocks, deep graven, there still is found the figure of the Cross. Go back to the Fourth Race of men, swallowed up by a mighty catastrophe, from which only the seed came over from which the Fifth Race was to spring; even there you will find the same symbol, sacred to the Fourth Race as it has been ever sacred to the Fifth. So that we may take it as a universal symbol, one that we cannot permit one of the latest and most modern of religions to usurp as though it belonged only to it. For it is a symbol often stamped on the breast of the Initiates, sacred to religion in its deepest recesses, and not the private property of one of the most modern and exoteric of faiths. Take then the Cross—what is it fundamentally? It was in the circle always in the oldest records; in later times the circle has fallen away from it, and the Cross, losing the circle, became degraded from its loftiest significance. Always the symbol has its highest meaning in the Spirit; and from the spiritual sphere it comes downward into outer manifestation and finds a second explanation in the stars which are the outer forms of the great Intelligences, by which the Kosmos moves; and then lower still it falls, until it comes down to man, and then it becomes more degraded in its latest phallic signification, polluted by the impure thoughts that flow to it from the mind in man. Take then the circle, and in its earliest significance it stands for that Boundless Existence which, coming into manifestation, circumscribes Itself. First, we have been taught of a circle of light, bounded by darkness which has no limit; and the circle of light is the beginning of the manifested Kosmos. Thus we found in studying light that first we had light without form, and then later form came as the visible side of the manifestation; and the circle in its earliest significance means manifestation, therefore limitation, the beginning of things. The Cross which, as the next stage, divides it is that fire which, flashing from the centre outwards, makes two diameters, gives active life within this circle of the universe, and makes possible the evolution which from the centre is gradually to proceed. At first, one line of the Cross is the line drawn in both directions by the light of the Logos from the centre outwards to the circumference—that light of the Logos that I spoke of in the second lecture, as shining out from the dual Logos, from that which we saw as Fire and Water, that which is Spirit-Matter, shining out from the centre which is the unmanifested Logos; this, passing outwards to the circumference, divides the circle first into two and then into four. It is this line of light starting from the point, passing outwards in the four directions, that traces the first Cross in manifestation, the symbol of the division into Spirit and Matter.[1] Then coming down a little further and recognizing this division of Spirit and Matter, there is the generation of the Kosmos, which is symbolized by the revolution of the Cross, so that the Cross is no longer two straight lines, but to each arm of the Cross there is attached a part of the circle of manifestation, and you get the ancient Svastika, which gives not only the idea of division, but also the idea of revolution. In the Svastika, with the limbs turned, there is a suggestion of the circle as well as of the Cross, but no longer of the circle set and steady, but of the circle revolving, having therefore become a generating

1 A student given to meditation may contemplate Point and Line, Cross, Svastika, and study the connection of these with the Three Logoi.

force of life. Closely united with this is the symbolism of the fire-sticks; here you have a socket which stands for the circle, and the upright stick which is made to revolve by a cord (thus forming a Cross) which, turning it round and round in the socket, generates fire, which is sacred, so giving birth to Agni the Fire-God, as the sign of that Life by which only the universe can appear. Thus you have not only the circle, not only the upright stick which represents half the Cross, but also the string which completes the Cross and causes revolution. There is the completed image of the second Logos by whose division further manifestation becomes possible. Then with the revolution, then with the heat which is generated—to which you may remember I drew your attention, as the result of this action of fire—when the mere radiance of light passes into fire, it is then you get the birth of the Fire-God, without whose generating influence no further manifestation may come. Then you can trace it downwards and downwards, through slight changes in the outer form, until you find it as everywhere symbolical of the God, of the God in manifestation, an essentially creative and productive power in the universe in its highest sense; in its highest sense the God that generates the Kosmos. In its lowest sense it is the representative of the reproductive organ, that too often gives rise to forms of exoteric worship which have become a degradation. The blinded eye of the Materialist reads but the phallic meaning, and reads into it his own impure signification; whereas that is the lowest point of materiality, while the highest is that which begins in the Logos itself, manifesting itself in the world of form. Thus tracing the Cross we find it in ancient sculptures in the hands of the Gods, constantly present, shaped slightly differently according to the type adopted by the people in their religion. There again there is another use of this symbolical language, for, according to the particular shape the symbol has assumed, we are able to judge of the stage to which the religion of that people has evolved. Take, for instance, the Egyptian religion; there you will find the Cross and the circle changed in appearance. The Cross is no longer the Cross which is traced on the circle of Time, with its two arms of equal length. It has become the letter T with one arm below the other, and instead of being within the circle of Time, the circle has gone outside it and rests on the top of the Tau. The circle is no longer Time, it stands for the female principle. In the hands of the Gods you may see it traced in the frescoes on the pyramids; you will find it there held as a symbol of human life; and when the mummy is lying prone and the time comes for the Soul to revivify it, then the God comes forward with this Tau and circle in his hand, the Cross of Life, and he touches with it the lips of the mummy and thus restores the Soul and brings the body to resurrection, to the possibility of renewed life. Instead of taking it in the later Egyptian religion, where it has fallen from its highest significance, let us take it in the hand of one of the Hindû Gods, and you will find that a subtler and a more beautiful significance may be drawn from it. Take the image of Shiva, Mahâ-deva, as you will find Him sometimes represented in the temples—represented as the Mahâ-Yogî, the great Ascetic, who by Tapas burned up everything that was of the lower nature and remained as Fire only; everything else having disappeared. The Mahâ-Yogî holds in His uplifted hand a cord—a cord that assumes an oval shape and not a circle—and He holds that in His uplifted hand, between the thumb and the fingers; and you will see that the oval rises above the hand, and that the hand makes the figure of the Cross on which this oval is supported. What can be the meaning in the hand of the great Yogî, the patron of all ascetics, what can be the meaning of this symbol, which in more modern literature has been taken as the productive symbol, the symbol of life? Has not the Yogî turned aside from this creative activity, for he is often symbolized by the virgin Kumâra, who has refused to create and who has nought to do with physical manifestation? The symbol has a loftier meaning. No longer does that oval in the hand of the great Ascetic convey to the mind of one versed in symbolism the later signification which was attached to it; it stands for the third eye of the

Spirit, for that which is opened by Tapas, that which is opened within the brain of the ascetic when a certain stage has been reached, at which the lower forces are conquered for evermore. For the hand that forms the Cross stands as a symbol for that crucifixion of the passions of the lower nature by which only the Yogî may attain spiritual life; and the God who is the great Yogî has His uplifted hand in this position to show that every passion has been crucified, and so, by the crucifixion of the lower, the opening of the higher has become possible. Thus the Cross becomes the means of opening the door by which the light of the Spirit may stream out, and then comes the opening of the third eye, which is the Eye of Shiva, familiar to every Hindû in name if not in understanding. And that third eye—how did it show itself? Remember once more the ancient story that, as He sat engaged in Tapas, the Hindû God of Love strove to shoot his shafts at Him, but the forehead of Shiva opened, and from the third eye shot forth a ray of light which burned the tempting God to ashes. For when that eye is opened, none of the lower passions may venture to approach the ascetic who has achieved. And whenever, passing into the temple of the great God, you see him represented as the Mahâ-Yogî, then look you for the cord and realize its inner significance.

You may go a step further, and take to yourself the lesson that there is conveyed, that in man there is a power which may be used for the lower or for the higher life, either for the creation of new forms or for the evolution of spiritual life in man, but not for both; and therefore celibacy has been the note of the ascetic, a necessary preliminary before the third eye can be opened. Therefore always the idea of the ascetic includes this idea of absolute physical purity. Either you may drive the life current upwards towards Spirit, or you may drive it downwards towards Matter. If it seeks its expression in the material, it cannot at the same time rise up into the mightier creative energies of the spiritual sphere. And when Shiva upraises this Cross and cord which symbolize the opening of the third eye, it means that the life has been centred in the head, that the third eye of the ascetic has been opened, and by that centreing at the higher pole the triumph of the Spirit is secured. You no longer have the downward tendency to Matter, you have achieved the triumph of the Spirit.

Let us seek the meaning of another symbol, in which Matter and Spirit are expressed, no longer divided but united. Here you have not the Cross and the oval but a double Triangle interlaced, showing that they are not to be separated, and so conveying to our thought the manifested universe and the union of Spirit and Matter in every possibility of phenomenal life. For here we have the Triangle upward pointing, which is fire or Spirit, and then the Triangle downward pointing, which is water or

Matter, and the union of the two inseparable. This means the union of Spirit and Matter in the manifested universe; and the fact is that that union remains so long as manifestation endures. You will find this double Triangle used to symbolize two of the Hindû Gods, used as a symbol of Shiva, and used as a symbol of Vishnu; this is when these are regarded as two aspects of the One. The upward pointing aspect is taken as that of Mahâdeva, that is fire; when He moves upon the waters, Nârâyana takes this symbol of the downward pointing Triangle to show the Deity evolving Matter, and so making phenomenal manifestation possible. So you again get the symbol of duality, in which you have the two Gods represented as one in Their essence, and only two in Their manifestation—fire and water, positive and negative, male and female, once again. That, to some of you, may throw light on an obscure suggestion that you may find in the Scriptures as to this inner relationship between the two great Gods of the Hindû faith.

Once more, in studying this, the story may come back to your mind that ought always to strike at the root of all bitterness between the modern sects —I use the word modern in comparison—who make the names of the Gods dividing walls, instead of uniting forces. For you may remember how a Shaivite worshipping in his temple felt a bitter hatred towards a neighbour that worshipped Vishnu, and worshipped, not in true religious spirit, but in antagonism to the other, whose chosen aspect of the God was different from his own. But lo! one day as he bowed before Mahâdeva with the thought of anger in his heart against him who worshipped Vishnu, the image before him changed in aspect; it no longer stood there as Shiva only, but it divided in twain; one side remained in the form of Mahâdeva, while the other side took the form of Vishnu, and the two together, no longer twain but one, smiled at the worshipper. If in modern times that story were understood, we should not see strife between two sects who worship one God under different aspects, and who should feel themselves as brothers, with no possibility of contention between them at all. And so studying these symbols, we come to the realization of the Divine in them, and to a clearer understanding of what underlies the outer form.

That leads me, following the same line of thought, to a more concrete kind of symbol. I take a concrete one on purpose, so that I may trace it in its evolution and show to you how the abstract idea which is most congenial to the highly educated mind, gradually emerges from a symbol that is more concrete, a symbol necessary if religion is to be made intelligible to the unlearned and to the ignorant. Here you will permit me to say one word a little aside perhaps from the subject, but not aside from the controversies which are rending India to-day. There is no commoner attack made upon India in the West than what is called an attack on its idolatry, and you will constantly find bitter jeers and scoffs uttered by people who have been over here, who have seen idols and idol-worship, and ceremonies performed to the idol, but who have never understood them —nay, who have never taken the trouble to try and understand them, nor even to ask the worshipper what to him is conveyed by such doings. These visitors, looking at the outside with the prejudice engendered by foreign feelings, go back to their own land, and then from many a platform speak of the poor Indians as heathen, given over to idolatry, who ought to be taught a more spiritual religion, and rescued from this degradation that presses on their minds and hearts. Now this matter of idolatry is a very important one, because it turns on this most essential question—shall there or shall there not be accommodation to Ignorance? How may religion be made at once the teacher of the most degraded and also the object of reverence to the most highly instructed and the most aspiring minds? It is a hard problem to deal with, for that which is fit for the education of the ignorant is not fit for the philosopher and for the highly evolved thinker. The symbolism that teaches the one is repellent to the other, and if you are going to say that religion shall be exactly the same for one and all, then there are only two possibilities before you. If religion is to be one and the same for all, you must bring it to the limit of the very lowest intellect and of the least developed understanding; otherwise they will be shut out. If it is to be the same for all, the philosopher must come down to the level of the labourer or the child, and his noblest aspirations must find no grander vehicle than that which is capable of being grasped by the most thoughtless and the most uninstructed of the people. On the other hand, if religion is to be useful to all, then you must permit differences to come into it—differences of presentation, according to the mind that is to be met. You must have a religion philosophic for the philosopher and childish for the child—not because thereby you would drag down religion, but in order that you may lift up the childish mind, and train it for the possibility of future evolution, which may raise it to the greatest height of religious thought. Now in the West a different method has been adopted. In the West it has been attempted to make religion "so simple that a costermonger can understand it." In England that word implies, as a rule, the very lowest intellectual ability and training, a man in the street with a barrow, selling vegetables, who will be the representative of the outcaste amongst yourselves. I was once told that Theosophy can never be useful, because it is beyond the grasp of the costermonger. What has been the effect on religious thought in Europe of thus lowering the intellectual side of religion? Its effect has been that the intellect of the people has gone outside religion; you have a complete divorce between intellect and religion, and the greatest minds refuse any longer to accept a religion that outrages their highest aspirations, and in which they can find no food for lofty spiritual emotions. That is the price which is paid for the dragging down of the Divine Ideal, so that it may be grasped by the most ignorant mind.

In India you have the other plan. You have the recognition that men's minds are in different stages of evolution, that that which is true for the villager in his field is not true for the Brâhman in his place of meditation. Both have rights in the religious world, and both have the possibility of the Spirit more or less evolved, therefore each should be fed with the food suitable for its evolution. You should no more feed the baby in intellect with the food of the man, than you should feed the baby in body with the food which is intended to support a man in his maturity. But that view means what is called idolatry; that means that you preserve the highest spirituality at the price of being misjudged by those who will not go underneath the outer sign of the idol. For the idol has different meanings according to the mind which the worshipper brings to it. The idol of the villager may be nothing more than some elemental form, to which he bows down, and to which he brings a drop of water or a flower, to which he strikes a bell. To the Brâhman, worship of such a Deity would be degrading, but it means to that villager something that he is able to recognize and to worship; and the worshipping act on his part, the love and the faith that stir in him will open out the way for spiritual life. If you gave him the abstract thought of the Brâhman, he would stand with open mouth, understanding nothing of its meaning; and you then would not stir in his heart the first faint throbbings of spiritual life. Let him have his idol which will be able to appeal to him, although it would be to you a degradation to worship it, and let the first quiver of spiritual life move within him. It will justify itself, it will begin his spiritual evolution, and, life after life, it will carry him onward to a higher, higher, and still higher view of Deity, until the Soul which began with the ringing of a bell before an Elemental shall find its home at the Lotus Feet of Mahâdeva, lost in the radiance that ever flows therefrom. That is what becomes possible when you realize that the Soul is trained through many lives. If you have only one life and then for ever after what is called Heaven, you must hurry everything on: otherwise it is clear that when the Soul gets to Heaven it will find itself in a perfectly incomprehensible position.

In order to show you how this idolatry may be used, let me take, as I have taken elsewhere, an image that will be familiar to you: the image of Mahâdeva on Nandi, His vehicle, the Bull. Now in a town when a day of festival comes, the image of the God is placed on this His vehicle, and is drawn through the streets of the town. It will be seen by many men whose minds are in different stages of evolution; to them it will convey different kinds of ideas. Let us first take the *Chhândogyopanishad* and the meanings which are given in that.[1] Brâhman is there spoken of as sitting on the Bull, but I take the more familiar form of Mahâdeva on Nandi. What does it mean, taking it from the popular standpoint? I am now merely quoting. The sky is symbolized by the God, and the man who is called the theological worshipper will simply see the outer image of the over-arching sky, which to him is a most effective symbol of greatness and grandeur; for, than the sky which has in itself the sun, the moon and the stars—what more impressive symbol can you possibly have, what which would convey to the limited mind the idea of infinity, of the boundless life which fills all space? So to him, if he has been taught something at least of the meaning of symbols, the God will stand for the over-arching sky; and the Bull on which He rides will be the symbol of the world; and the four feet of the Bull, each of them having a special name, will tell him something of the way in which the world or the universe moves. For one foot will be Agni or fire, another foot will be Vâyu or the God of wind—the Great Breath, in

[1] Ch. iii. sec. XVIII. 1.

higher parlance, of the Supreme; another foot will be the Sun, as it shines, giving light to the world, and the fourth foot will be the quarters or the divisions of the sky. So to his mind these would be conveyed by this symbol, if some one would explain to him the idea of the over-arching care of the Divine, resting on the manifested world, and the sun, the fire, the wind and the quarters in the sky, all symbolized in these feet of the Bull that carry onward the God, and so support and guide the life of the manifested universe. Then some of you will seek after a subtler explanation that will be given you; and this is called the intellectual worship. Then the God will be the mind in man, and the God riding on His vehicle will be the mind dwelling in the body. Then the feet of the Bull will not have lost their significance, for one foot will be speech, another foot will be breath, another will be vision, and another will be the hearing. And then Shankarâchârya teaches that as the four feet of the Bull carry the animal wherever it desires to go, so does mind attain its objects through speech, breath, vision and hearing, which bring the body and the Soul within it into contact with the outer and material universe. Thus by means of these feet of the Bull, the senses of the man, there may be carried inwards to the Soul the knowledge which the Soul has come into manifestation to seek. So you have your philosophic meaning of the idol as it passes through the streets, and it reminds you of the embodied Soul. And there is yet a deeper meaning that you will not find thus plainly given, but which you may work out for yourself or at least recognize when I give the explanation. Now let the God stand for the Divine itself, for the Spirit that we seek, for the highest manifestation—call It Brâhman, call It Shiva, call It Vishṅu, give It what name you will; but recognize the One, the All, the Indivisible, symbolized under this name and under this idol form. What then will mean the feet of the Bull? They will mean states of consciousness, whereby the Soul may climb upwards towards its Lord; so that foot after foot of the Bull shall be state after state of the Soul by which it comes nearer and nearer to the universal Spirit, until at last it shall find itself one with It. One foot will be the waking state in which the Soul lives and moves in its waking hours; the next foot will mean the Svapna state that we spoke of yesterday, which in the Soul is taken as a second step towards the Divine; the third foot will mean the Sushupti state, where one step more is taken towards the Divinity; and the last foot will mean the Turîya state, from which the Soul passes onward into unity with God. So that the loftiest conception of the spiritual Philosophy is brought to the developed mind when that symbol is seen. Thus I myself, familiar with this loftier view, constantly having that in mind, had it brought back to my outer consciousness with intensity and vividness, when walking through the temple of Madura, I saw an image, a sculptured form of the Sacred Bull, which became to my mind not a mere bull, carved in stone, but a voice that recalled the teaching that I had received of the states of consciousness, and reminded me of the upward path which ended in the God. Thus you may take what is called the idol and find in it what you bring to it; and if you have no spiritual life within you, which brings to it its real signification, you have no right to simply scoff at idolatry, which is empty to you only because you are empty.

So again you may take the *Purânas*, full of symbolism of the most complicated and difficult kind. If you want to understand how that symbolism may be explained, turn to a single question that you find dealt with in Madame Blavatsky's *Secret Doctrine;* and in the method of unravelling of one myth, you may possibly gain the key which may enable you to unlock for yourself many another mystery. I am only taking one out of a very large number of instances which she takes from the Paurânic stories, explaining their different meanings. The one that I select and to which I wish to draw your attention, and which I will not work out in detail, for you can read it for yourself, is that of the Maruts[1]—the Gods of the wind and the children of Rudra, the Roarer, signifying the tones and the force of the wind manifested in phe-

1 *Secret Doctrine*, ii. 631, etc., *n.e.* 648, etc.

nomenal shape. First of all that represents a fact in Nature. It represents the fact that behind every force in Nature there is an intelligence, that every natural phenomenon has an entity connected with it, so that in the plainest sense and the most obvious signification, these Maruts are entities that deal with certain forms of manifestation in the phenomenal universe; and if you understand them, their language and their powers, then the phenomena they control become subject to your knowledge. To no evolved spirit will the Maruts be objects of worship; they will be powers that he controls by his own will; no Rishi would worship the Maruts, he would command them; but that does not alter the fact that they are real entities, that they have their real place in the Kosmos, that they are among the Devas, who are the spirit-side of every physical phenomenon that you see; and if you lose that fundamental truth of Occultism, and if in studying the physical phenomena you see the phenomena only and not the Spirit that controls, then you are simply blinding yourselves to the real lessons of Nature, and Matter has achieved over Spirit its last triumph, for not only does it conceal Spirit from physical vision, but also it conceals it from the Spirit that is in man. The Maruts then in their lowest signification are entities—entities connected with the atmospheric world, immediately connected with the production of winds and under subjection to the trained and purified will in man.

Then there is another signification, in which you find them no longer as those entities in the Kosmos, but in their character as the children of Rudra—that Rudra who once more is Shiva and once more the Mahâ-Yogî. What then cân be the signification of the children of the Yogî, the children of the Virgin Ascetic? They become then the passions of his nature, they symbolize the forces which he has mastered, and they become, from this standpoint, the enemies of man, striving at first against him; and then going higher, still keeping this symbolism of the ascetic, those which were his children of the lower nature, the passions that he had to conquer: they become the children of the higher nature, when the lower has been conquered by the purified will of the ascetic in which all power resides, and by them he may work in the external universe. Then you come to the story in which Indra tries to destroy them, for the child is to be born who is to destroy Indra himself, and Indra in this sense is the lower manifestation of Nature—the God of the sky, the bearer of the thunderbolt, symbolizing a manifested and physical Kosmos; and as the child to be born shall destroy him (once again, the Marut), Indra casts forth his thunderbolt, and in the womb he shivers the embryo into seven pieces, which again are divided seven-fold. It is the lower that has checked the development of the higher, and has turned into lower forms the forces that ought to have grown into the developed and purified will. And so, step by step, bringing together all the different symbols that you may find scattered through the *Purânas*, you will find that this conception of the Maruts may be translated into most instructive suggestions which may guide you in your own transmutation of your lower forces into higher, and the change of Kâma, that physically creates, into a desire which in the Spirit is the source of all progress and the spring of all true life. I mention this particular case, because many of you may be inclined to study the matter—I ought not perhaps to say many—but if you desire to carry on the study further, you will find, if you will use this great teacher, H. P. Blavatsky, who was sent to us, as you ought to use her, that is, by studying the knowledge that she was given to convey to us, and using it as a clue to further knowledge, you may do for the world a service whose value it is impossible to estimate. You may take your own Scriptures with an accuracy of knowledge which she did not possess; you may take them in their original form in Sanskrit, a language that she had not mastered; and you may get from them in that language, the language of the Gods, using the light that she has placed in your hands, many an inner meaning and many a secret clue; then you may give these to the world and so carry on this work which she was sent here to begin and not to finish. For it is hoped by those who sent her that if a stimulus were given, there might be here and there a man amongst the Indian people who would spring forward to the light, and taking it from her hand would carry it onwards, and bring out of these ancient Scriptures a spiritual teaching, which is needed for the helping of the world. If there should be one man here who was inspired by this suggestion to study for himself, I should count it that her life had borne here its true fruit; for her reward would be really won only if an impulse were given to the spiritual life of the world.

And so I might take you through many another symbol, so I might point out to you many another thing. Let me take what appears so simple a case —a Brâhman's thread. What does it symbolize? What ought it to represent? It symbolizes the triple nature of man, the lower, the middle and the higher; it symbolizes those three planes of consciousness of which I spoke yesterday; it symbolizes the three conditions of Âtmâ, of which also I spoke; it symbolizes in addition to these the body, speech and mind. Take those significations, and then judge what it ought to mean when a man wears it. The world knows who wears it, and to eyes that are trained that outer symbol is either sanctified or desecrated according as it represents a reality or a lie. For first of all as regards body, speech and mind, it symbolizes the control of each; and therefore when the knots are tied in it, it means that the man who wears the thread has gained control over body, speech and mind. It conveys to the eye that sees it the idea of a man of perfect self-control, whose body can never betray him and whose senses can never conquer him; whose speech can never soil nor hurt one ear on which it falls, whose speech will be self-controlled, used only when there is something to be said which is worth saying, never used for an unkind word, for the Brâhman is the friend of all creatures and his speech must always help and must never wound. And not only does it symbolize the man thus controlled in body and speech, but also it implies that control of the mind has been achieved, and that the mind is held by the grip of the triple cord with its knots upon it, so that it may serve as a helper to the highest that is in him, and be used for the service of men to whom the Brâhman belongs. For the Brâhman has no right of existence for himself; he lives for the people and not for himself. If he lives for himself he is not a true Brâhman; he may have the outer signs of caste, he may have the triple cord, he may use the sacred name, and he may even obey the rules of his order; but these are only the outer shell. Only if he lives not for himself but for the world, is he of the Brâhman caste, standing as the spiritual servant, which in the world he was to be. He came from the mouth of Brahmâ that he might be the spoken word of the divine life among men.

That is the meaning of the Brâhman. Whenever I see the thread, I think to myself whether it is a reality or not—does it represent a truth, or is it only the survival of an ancient custom which has become the worst of blasphemies? For the degradation of the highest to the lowest is the worst of degradations, it is the poisoning of the world, for it poisons the spiritual life in man. These words may seem strong, but they are of that spirit on which the ancient Scriptures are based. They are no stronger than Manu spoke; they are no stronger than may be found in such writings as the *Mahâbhârata;* they are no stronger than may be read in many a *Purâna;* and if they seem a bitter irony to-day, as I know they do, it is because I am speaking the words of the old world in the modern world, and the contrast between theory and practice is too startling. Since, however, the theory is true, I, while still an outcaste, recognizing the fact, make no claim amongst you. I have none in my present condition, and I give outward recognition to that caste which ought to manifest the holiness of the Brâhman. That is why I say that if India is to be regenerated, it must come from this caste that symbolizes her past, and therefore has in it the promise of her future, no matter what it may be to-day; that is why, when I am asked to initiate reforms, I answer: "Let me serve you with suggestion, with help, if you will, but let the leadership in reform belong to the spiritual caste which has the right of leadership, so that in coming it may come without destruction, without shivering the very foundation on which the future life of the people is to be builded."

I who say these things may seem to press unfairly on you, for you are not personally to blame that the whole land has fallen; you as individuals are a part of a great nation, and you with it have gone downwards. But what shall I say to you, my Brâhman brothers, you whom I ought to be able to address as fathers? If I cannot do so, it is because I know in many things more than you do; I, an outcaste, who ought to sit at your feet as your pupil, cannot do so, because you have not the knowledge to give me which the pupil has a right to claim from the teacher if he bows down before him. I appeal to you, you of the spiritual caste, to uphold it, and to recognize its present degradation. And if I speak these words which seem to make a bitter contrast, it is because in your hands lies the spiritual future of these people, because though the whole nation has fallen and you have fallen with it, yet in you there is still the power that ought to be able to begin the upward path; and though success will only be by the toil of many generations, there is no reason why you should not begin to-day. I know too well that in a moment you cannot do it, and I know that for the time your cord must remain a mockery, and the nobler you are the bitterer the irony you will feel in wearing it, because you know what it represented and how it has fallen. I say that not in reproach, for who am I that I should reproach you? I say it in order that here and there amongst you a desire for higher life may be born, for I would send, even as by a thunderbolt, into your hearts the bitterness of the degradation, so that the possibility of rising upwards may be realized once more amongst men. For I would that each of you, feeling the degradation and recognizing it, should not cast off the sacred cord, but begin to purify the life and thus justify its wearing; and if only in small things a beginning were made, the first upward step would be taken. For there are many lives before us, life after life that stretches in front of you, a mighty caste not able now to live up to its glorious traditions. And therefore I say, let us take up the cup of our Karma, let us bear it onward bravely as brave men should bear, not quarrelling with its weight inasmuch as we have made it ourselves in the past; recognizing it as bitter, let us drink it, and in drinking it, let its bitterness purify the soul, that we may gain strength to change to all that we long for, and may be resolute to alter ourselves, and so the spiritual purification of the people also shall begin. Then when we come back to birth, as we shall come swiftly if our desire is to help the people to whom we belong, then we shall find things a little better, and in that better life we shall be able to work hand in hand when the triple cord will have lost the mockery between the wearing and the meaning, and so life after life we shall lift the whole of this people that has fallen in our fall, and will rise in our rise.

That is my last word to you in this hall, not a word of reproach but a word of common sorrow, and of common aspiration for this Hindû nation. We are responsible for it. Let us then begin the work of reformation, and from generation to generation we shall work until India shall rise step after step, and we shall place her again where she ought to be and where in truth she always is—at the feet of the Great Gods. Though the people do not see her there now, they shall see her there then; and then the light that springs from the Lotus Feet shall envelope her, so that the world shall worship her, and know that she is indeed the Spirit in the body of Humanity.